ABOUT THE OSTRAINING EVERYTHING CLUB

Local Web Development with DDEV Explained is part of the OSTraining Everything Club.

The club gives you access to

- all of our video classes
- all of the "Explained" books

Because we self-publish, we can release timely updates. Our books are active. We don't do long, boring explanations, and you don't need any prior experience to understand the material. The books are suitable even for complete beginners.

Join the OSTraining Everything Club today by visiting our website at https://ostraining.com. You'll be able to download ebook copies of "Local Web Development With DDEV Explained," as well as, our other books and videos.

WE OFTEN UPDATE THIS BOOK

This is version 1.4 of *Local Web Development With DDEV Explained*. This version was released in June of 2021.

WHAT'S NEW IN VERSION 1.4 (DDEV-LOCAL 1.16.2)

- Removed the Drud team image from the "DDEV-Local Explained" chapter for easier updates.
- Updated Mac OS X requirements and completely rewrote the Windows installation instructions in "Installing DDEV-Local Explained" chapter.
- Completely re-wrote the Windows installation instructions and added information about using Composer 2 in the "Installing a New Drupal Site in DDEV-Local Explained" chapter.
- Added the ability to use PHP 8 and new commands for CMS command line tools in the "Useful DDEV-Local Tips and Tricks Explained" chapter.
- Added "sequelace" and "tableplus" information to the "The Basics of DDEV-Local Explained" chapter.
- Removed mentions of Drupal Console in multiple chapters.
- Added new/updated config.yaml configuration options to the appendix.
- Added Magento and Laravel mentions in "DDEV-Local Explained" chapter.
- Update Mac OS X requirements for Docker for Mac in the "Installing DDEV-Local Explained" chapter.
- Updated example to use Drupal 9 in "Installing a New Drupal Site in DDEV-Local Explained" chapter.

- Updated information about the "ddevdemo" project codebase in the "Cloning an Existing Drupal Site to DDEV-Local Explained" chapter.

- Removed "ddev auth-pantheon" command in lieu of "ddev auth pantheon" command in the "Integrating DDEV-Local with a Hosting Provider" chapter.

- Added information about Pantheon's Terminus command-line tool in the "Integrating DDEV-Local with a Hosting Provider" chapter.

- Standardized on "ddev stop" instead of "ddev remove".

- Added "ddev launch -p" and "ddev launch -m" information in the "Using the Most Common DDEV-Local Commands" chapter.

- Added new "Extend DDEV's Web Container Explained" chapter.

- Added "ddev xdebug on" and "ddev xdebug off" commands in the "Using DDEV-Local with Xdebug and PhpStorm Explained" chapter.

- Updated information about PHP_IDE_CONFIG environment variable in the "Using DDEV-Local With Xdebug and PhpStorm Explained" chapter.

- Added "disable_settings_management", removed "webcache_enabled" DDEV-Local settings in Appendix.

WHAT'S NEW IN VERSION 1.3 (DDEV-LOCAL 1.12.0)

- Updated Windows installer instructions in the "Installing DDEV-Local Explained" chapter.

- Updated DDEV command list in "The Basics of DDEV-Local Explained" chapter as well as at the end of most chapters.

- Added new drupal/recommended-project content in the "Installing a New Drupal Site in DDEV-Local Explained" chapter.
- Added "ddev mysql", "ddev stop —unlist", and "ddev poweroff" commands to "Using the Most Common DDEV-Local Commands" chapter.
- Added .ddev/homeadditions/ example, updated PHP version information, "ddev debug" command, and omitting the database container at a project level to "Useful DDEV-Local Tips and Tricks Explained" chapter.
- Added DDEV custom command example to renamed "Extending and Creating Custom DDEV-Local Commands Explained" chapter.
- Added updated PHP, MySql, and MariaDB version information and webimage_extra_package example in the appendix.
- Rewrote the "Integrating Apache Solr With Drupal and DDEV-Local Explained" chapter, removing Drupal 7-related content and updating for the 8.x-3.x version of the Search API Solr module.

WHAT'S NEW IN VERSION 1.2 (DDEV-LOCAL 1.9.1)

- Added section on config.*.yaml files in the "Useful DDEV-Local Tips and Tricks Explained" chapter.
- Added host_db_port and host_webserver_port to DDEV-Local config.yaml options section in Appendix.
- Clarified Pantheon project machine name in "Integrating DDEV-Local with a Hosting Provider" chapter.
- Added "ddev exec enable/disable_xdebug" note to Xdebug chapter.

- Updated Solr chapter to reflect code changes.
- Added section on NFS mounting in the "Useful DDEV-Local Tips and Tricks Explained" chapter.
- Added information about installing and upgrading DDEV-Local on Windows 10 using Chocolately.
- Added section on using mkcert in the "Useful DDEV-Local Tips and Tricks Explained" chapter.
- Added "ddev pause" to "Using the Most Common DDEV-Local Commands".
- Streamlined ddev start, stop, remove, pause command explanations.
- Updated list of packages installed in containers by default in Appendix.
- Updated config.yaml options in Appendix.
- Updated Command Hooks chapter with new hooks.
- Updated everywhere to use "*.ddev.site" instead of "*.ddev.local".
- Added new chapter on "ddev share".

WHAT'S NEW IN VERSION 1.1 (DDEV-LOCAL 1.5.2)

- Added "Installing a new WordPress site in DDEV-Local Explained" chapter.
- Added "Cloning an Existing WordPress Site to DDEV-Local Explained" chapter.
- Added "Packages installed in DDEV default containers", "DDEV config.yaml options", and "DDEV-Local project configuration anatomy" sections to Appendix chapter.
- Added "How to use Apache instead of nginx in the "web" container" and "How to disable the "dba" container" to the

"Useful DDEV-Local Tips and Tricks Explained" chapter.

- Added a bit about the "file" command to the "Cloning an Existing Drupal Site to DDEV-Local Explained" chapter.
- Updated the "How to Export a Database" section of the "Useful DDEV-Local Tips and Tricks Explained" chapter.
- Moved "ddev ssh" intro to "Using the Most Common DDEV-Local Commands" chapter.
- Updated the "Installing a New Site in DDEV-Local Explained" chapter with the new (and awesome) "ddev composer" command.
- Added a "ddev auth ssh" section to the "Useful DDEV-Local Tips and Tricks Explained" chapter.
- Added a section on "ddev composer" to "Using the Most Common DDEV-Local Commands" chapter.
- Updated the "DDEV commands" list at the end of all chapters.
- Fixed –projectname -> —project-name and —project type -> —project-type issue in "Installing a new site" chapter.
- Changed the title of "Installing a New Site in DDEV-Local Explained" to "Installing a New Drupal Site in DDEV-Local Explained".
- Added bit about using the WordPress command line tool in the "Useful DDEV-Local Tips and Tricks Explained" chapter.
- Added info about support for PHP 7.3, MariaDB 10.1.
- Added "Global DDEV-Local Settings" section in "Useful DDEV-Local Tips and Tricks Explained" chapter.
- Added section about working offline to the tips and tricks chapter.
- Modified Linux installation and upgrades using

Linuxbrew.
- Added section about keeping Docker happy to Tips and Tricks chapter.

ADVANTAGES AND DISADVANTAGES

We often release updates for this book. Most of the time, frequent updates are wonderful. If the software makes a change in the morning, we can have a new version of this book available in the afternoon. Most traditional publishers wait years and years before updating their books.

There are two disadvantages to be aware of:

- Page numbers do change. We often add and remove material from the book to reflect changes in the software.
- There's no index at the back of this book. This is because page numbers do change, and also because our self-publishing platform doesn't have a way to create indexes yet. We hope to find a solution for that soon.

Hopefully, you think that the advantages outweigh the disadvantages. If you have any questions, we're always happy to chat: books@ostraining.com.

THANK YOU TO OUR READERS

If you find anything that is wrong or out-of-date, please email us at books@ostraining.com. We'll update the book, and to say thank you, we'll provide you with a new digital copy.

ARE YOU A TEACHER?

We hope that many schools, colleges, and organizations will adopt Local Web Development with DDEV Explained as a teaching guide to DDEV.

This book is designed to be a step-by-step guide that students can follow at different speeds. The book can be used for a multi-day class or a longer class over multiple weeks.

If you are interested in teaching DDEV, we'd be delighted to help you with review copies, and all the advice you need.

Please email books@ostraining.com to talk with us.

Local Web Development With DDEV Explained

LOCAL WEB DEVELOPMENT WITH DDEV EXPLAINED

Your Step-by-Step Guide to Local Web Development With DDEV Explained

MICHAEL ANELLO

OSTraining, LLC

Houston, Texas

Local Web Development with DDEV Explained Copyright © 2021 by Michael Anello. All Rights Reserved.

DDEV is a product from Drud Technology, LLC.

Written by Michael Anello.
Edited by Robbie Adair & Mikall Angela Hill.
Cover design by OS Training, LLC.
Interior design by OS Training, LLC.

This book or any portion thereof may not be reproduced or used in any manner whatsoever without the express written permission of the publisher except for the use of brief quotations in a book review. Proper names and contact information are used as examples in this book. No association with any organization or individual is intended, nor should it be inferred.

This book is published by OS Training, LLC. All Rights Reserved.

First printing, 2017.

OS Training LLC
1127 Eldridge Parkway Ste 300-114
Houston, Texas 77077

www.ostraining.com

CONTENTS

PART I. WELCOME

PART II. DDEV-LOCAL EXPLAINED

1. Introducing Our Web Development Problem — 9
2. The Basics of DDEV-Local Explained — 12
3. Professional Development Workflows Explained — 17
4. Installing DDEV-Local Explained — 23
5. Installing a New Drupal Site in DDEV-Local Explained — 32
6. Installing a New WordPress Site in DDEV-Local Explained — 40
7. Cloning an Existing Drupal Site to DDEV-Local Explained — 56
8. Cloning an Existing WordPress Site to DDEV-Local Explained — 66
9. Integrating DDEV-Local with a Hosting Provider — 74
10. Using the Most Common DDEV-Local Commands — 83
11. Extending and Creating Custom DDEV-Local Commands Explained — 94

12.	Useful DDEV-Local Tips and Tricks Explained	101
13.	Integrating Apache Solr With Drupal and DDEV-Local Explained	125
14.	Extending DDEV-Local's Web Container Explained	137
15.	Share Your DDEV-Local Project Online Explained	147
16.	Using DDEV-Local With Xdebug and PhpStorm Explained	153
17.	What's Next?	168
	Appendix	171
	About the Author	178
	Are You an Author?	180
	We Want to Hear from You	181
	Sponsor an OSTraining Book	182

PART I.

WELCOME

As part of the long-form Drupal training classes I teach, I've been teaching folks how to set up and use a local development environment for their projects. Up until 2017, I've based those lessons on a rather old-school, all-in-one AMP stack, mainly for two reasons: firstly, so that I could teach students the same lessons regardless of their choice of operating system, and secondly so that we could get up-and-running quickly – without having to spend a week learning how to use Vagrant or some other complex tool.

THIS BOOK FOCUSES ON DDEV-LOCAL

I spent about a year looking for an alternative – focusing mainly on virtual machine-based solutions, but also keeping my eye on Docker-based tools. As Docker-based tools emerged, one rose to the top, and I made the jump to DDEV-Local. I updated my long-form curriculum to use DDEV-Local and haven't looked back since. In fact, I recently purchased a new local development machine, and so far, DDEV-Local is the only local development environment I've installed.

DDEV-Local is a relatively new tool, and it is rapidly evolving. I'll do my best to keep this book up-to-date, but be sure to utilize the online support options listed at the end of this book to help you continue on your journey. As of today, I have several more topics in mind that I'll be adding to future versions of this book, including using the DDEV user interface (*coming soon!*) as well as adding custom containers to your local projects.

As you'll read in the following chapters, I'm a firm believer in the use of a local development environment combined with a solid, best-practice-based developer workflow. I believe that DDEV-Local integrates perfectly into efficient, professional workflows, and I'm excited to introduce you to this tool.

If you love learning how to develop better, faster, or more elegantly, then, let's get started!

THINGS IN THIS BOOK WILL CHANGE

Software changes regularly, and so do the extra features and designs that you add on to it.

Everything in this book is correct at the time of writing. However, it's possible that some of the instructions and screenshots may become out-of-date.

Be patient with any changes you find. You can find updates and send errata via:

http://ostraining.com/books/local

Please feel free to visit that site, search for updates, and contact us if you find any we haven't listed. If you do send us errata, we'll update the book and send you a new copy.

WHAT DO YOU NEED FOR THIS BOOK?

Now that you know a little bit about this book, let's make sure you're ready to follow along.

You need only two things to follow along with the exercises in this book:

1. A computer with an Internet connection
2. A computer where you can install DDEV-Local

Yes, that's really all you need.

THANK YOU, REVIEWERS!

A number of folks have provided some amazing feedback to this book, for that I am most appreciative. Thank you Kyle Hall, Nathan Smith, and most of all, Randy Fay of Drud!

PART II.

DDEV-LOCAL EXPLAINED

Before you start using DDEV-Local, let's give you some background on DDEV-Local itself.

WHAT IS DDEV-LOCAL?

DDEV-Local is an open-source local development environment for PHP-based projects. Its focus is providing a robust and flexible local development environment for open-source content management systems like Drupal, WordPress, TYPO3 CMS, Laravel, and Magento. If you don't want to use a CMS, DDEV-Local also has support custom PHP projects.

DDEV-Local is designed mainly for PHP developers. Although DDEV-Local works with many platforms, the examples in this book will focus on using DDEV-Local with Drupal.

DDEV-Local uses Docker, a tool that allows developers to package up services in containers. The power behind Docker is that it provides a hardware-independent way of running containers, so that you can run any Docker container on any hardware that supports Docker. In a typical DDEV-Local scenario, there is a web server container, a database server container, and a database administration container. DDEV-Local provides you with reliable Docker containers and removes some of Docker's complexities. All-in-all, DDEV-Local provides an easy-to-use, flexible, and powerful local development environment.

Professional web developers should always be doing development in a local environment. However, there are both modern and old-fashioned approaches to local development. DDEV-Local is built on modern principles. If you use something like MAMP, WAMP, or XAMPP, then you should definitely consider modernizing your local development environment with DDEV-Local.

WHO IS THE TEAM BEHIND DDEV-LOCAL?

While DDEV-Local is an open-source project, it is backed by Drud Technology: https://www.ddv.com.

One of Drud's goals is to design a system that provides container-based development tools on both local (*DDEV-Local*) and remote environments – ideally with configurations and processes in place to be able to manage all environments concurrently.

In addition to this, Drud provides DDEV-Live, a hosting service that utilizes the same project environment configuration as DDEV-Local. Drud also provides consulting and support to development teams for end-to-end development-to-deployment workflows.

Members of the DDEV-Local team have been heavily involved in the Drupal and PHP community for many years.

WHAT ARE THE ALTERNATIVES TO DDEV-LOCAL?

If you're already a web developer, then you hopefully are already using a local development environment.

1. If you're on Mac OS X, then maybe you use MAMP, Acquia Dev Desktop, or you have installed a web and database server yourself using Homebrew.
2. If you're on Windows, you've probably used WAMP, XAMPP, or Acquia Dev Desktop.
3. If you're comfortable with virtual machines, perhaps you're using one of the many pre-build developer-focused solutions that can be found online.
4. If you're more on the forefront of new technology, maybe you're already using a Docker-based solution such as Lando, Docksal, Flight Deck, or similar.

WHY SHOULD YOU CHOOSE DDEV-LOCAL?

1. **Easy to get a site up-and-running.** Once DDEV-Local is installed, it takes only a few minutes to get an existing site up-and-running. With most projects, all you need to do is get the codebase, import the database, and you're good-to-go.
2. **Manageable command set.** The DDEV-Local set of commands is small and easy to use. There are less than five commands that you'll need to start, stop, and configure a new project with DDEV-Local.
3. **DDEV-Local support.** The DDEV-Local support options are numerous and up-to-date. Also, Drud team members on the official support channel are super-responsive. We talk more about support in the final chapter of this book, called "What's Next?"

4. **Built on Docker.** DDEV-Local is built on the solid, well-loved, well-maintained Docker platform. If DDEV-Local can't do something you want it to do , then you can usually find a workaround with a few Docker-based tweaks.

WHAT'S NEXT?

In this chapter, I just provided a brief introduction to what DDEV-Local is.

The next step is to make sure we're all on the same page as to what a professional developer workflow looks like and where DDEV-Local fits in.

CHAPTER 1.

INTRODUCING OUR WEB DEVELOPMENT PROBLEM

Now that we know a little bit about local development, let's start this book by defining the problem we face.

In this chapter, you'll learn about some of the reasons why managing local development environments can be complex and time-consuming. I'll then introduce DDEV-Local as a solution.

THE PROBLEM

The problem is that the modern web is evolving and becoming more complex. As a result, the software we need for developing web projects is also becoming more complicated.

In the old days, you only needed a web server, a database server, and your favorite scripting language.

However, now you need to think about your web server software, scripting languages, database servers, testing tools, front-end development tools, version control and more. Here's an overview of the tools I rely on for many projects:

1. Scripting language (*PHP, .NET, Python*)
2. Web server (*Apache, NGINX, IIS*)

3. Database server (*MariaDB, MySql, Postgresql*)
4. Search server (*Solr, Elasticsearch*)
5. Testing tools (*Behat, PHPSpec*)
6. Dependency managers (*Composer, NPM*)
7. Front-end toolchain (*Gulp, Grunt*)
8. Debugging tools (*Xdebug*)
9. Caching tools (*Redis, Memcache*)

That's a lot of set up and configuration! Imagine you've got all those tools set up for a customer. What about the next customer? And the next? And the next? Different customers have different requirements. In the morning, you may need to be developing in PHP on Apache with Composer. In the afternoon, you may need to be writing Javascript on NGINX.

Now imagine you are a project manager with a team of developers. With more projects, you may have to deal with dozens of different customers, each one requiring different tools. To make sure the project runs smoothly, you need to give your team the tools they need. And you need to make sure that your team's development environments are all configured the same way. How many times have you seen the "it works on my machine" problem?

Oh, and by the way, we're only talking about the development stage. You may be able to get your team of developers up-and-running with the tools they need for different customers. But what happens when it comes to deployment time? Your local environments often don't match your remote, testing and production environments.

So there's our problem.

THE SOLUTION

We need a tool that helps to manage the software and configuration for our local development environments.

DDEV-Local is that tool.

DDEV-Local allows you to customize a local development environment on a per-project basis. It also provides a way to codify and share the configuration, allowing all team members to utilize the same configuration. DDEV-Live extends this idea to remote environments.

DDEV-Local provides a solid local development environment for web-based projects. It replaces more traditional AMP stack solutions (*WAMP, MAMP, XAMPP, etc.*) with a more flexible, modern, Docker-based solution. With DDEV-Local, you can have a unique set of Docker containers for each project. These containers can include specific applications and versions of web servers, database servers, search index servers, and other types of software.

DDEV-Local offers a solution to the complexity of the modern web.

WHAT'S NEXT?

Now we have a general understanding of the problem and solution that I'm discussing in this book.

The next step is to achieve a deeper understanding. In the next chapter, I'll give you a detailed explanation of what a professional workflow should look like, and how you can achieve it with DDEV-Local.

CHAPTER 2.

THE BASICS OF DDEV-LOCAL EXPLAINED

In the last chapter, I explained why web developers need a tool like DDEV-Local.

Before we dive into specific examples of installing and using DDEV-Local, in this chapter, I'm going to explain some of the basic principles underlying DDEV-Local.

INTRODUCING DDEV-LOCAL CONTAINERS

If you've not used Docker before, it would be helpful to read this background on containers:

> https://www.docker.com/resources/what-container

The short version is that explanation is that "a container is a standard unit of software that packages up code and all its dependencies so the application runs quickly and reliably from one computing environment to another."

By default, a DDEV-Local project will provide three Docker containers for each project:

1. **web**: This includes NGINX and PHP. This is the container that the developer most often interacts with from the command line. The project root directory is

mounted with the host operating system.

2. **db (database):** This includes MariaDB. Unlike some other Docker-based local development environment solutions, the actual database data is stored in a Docker volume: https://docs.docker.com/storage/volumes/.

3. **dba (database administration):** This includes the phpMyAdmin database client.

DDEV-Local uses the concept of *mounting* a directory. This concept is not unique to Docker. The basic idea is that a directory on your development machine is *mounted* inside the Docker container so that both the host OS and the Docker container have access to it. The host OS and the Docker container aren't actually sharing the directory. Instead, the directory is synced from one to the other. Any changes made to any files, either by the host OS or from within the Docker container, are instantly synced with the other. The advantage of this approach is that you can use tools that are native to your host OS, such as code editors, and front-end tools.

INTRODUCING DDEV-LOCAL'S ENVIRONMENT CONFIGURATION

DDEV-Local's environment configuration is stored in a ".ddev/" directory on the project root. When you run the "ddev config" command, a ".ddev/config.yaml" file is created.

I recommend that you commit this ".ddev/" directory to your project's repository. This will make it easier to share the development environment configuration with your team members.

INTRODUCING DDEV-LOCAL COMMANDS

DDEV-Local has a set of commands you can use to interact with your local environment.

```
ddev [command]
```

Here are some example of the commands you can use:

1. **ddev config**: configure a project's containers
2. **ddev rm**: remove a project's containers
3. **ddev start**: start a project's containers
4. **ddev stop**: stop (and remove) a project's containers

Many of the commands have parameters and flags that you can use to modify the command. To view the available parameters and flags for each command, use this:

```
ddev [command] -h
```

Throughout this book, we're going to rely heavily on DDEV-Local commands. I've included a list of 29 commands that you'll see. At the end of each chapter, I will note which commands were covered.

1. **auth**: a collection of authentication commands
2. **composer**: run Composer commands in the "web" container
3. **config**: create or modify a DDEV set of containers
4. **debug**: a collection of debugging commands
5. **delete**: remove all project information including the database.
6. **describe**: output information about the current DDEV configuration

7. **exec**: execute a shell command in one of the project containers
8. **export-db**: exports a copy of the database to .sql format
9. **help**: get additional information about DDEV commands
10. **hostname**: add a hostname to the host operating system
11. **import-db**: import a database into the database container
12. **import-files**: extract and place content files in the proper directory
13. **launch**: opens the current site in the user's default browser
14. **list**: output a list of DDEV projects (*only those projects with containers currently built will be displayed*)
15. **logs**: access combined logs of currently running containers
16. **mysql**: opens a SQL command line for the current project's default database
17. **pause**: stops (*and does not remove*) a project's containers
18. **poweroff**: stops all DDEV projects and containers
19. **pull**: update local environment with database and content files from a remote provider
20. **restart**: restarts a project's containers
21. **restore-snapshot**: restores a project's database to a previously saved snapshot
22. **sequelpro**: Launch the Sequel Pro database client (*Mac OS X*) connected to the project's database. Similar commands exist for "sequelace" (*Mac OS X*) and "tableplus" (*multiple platforms*)
23. **share**: make your local project available via a public URL for testing and review

24. **snapshot**: creates a database snapshot
25. **ssh**: opens a shell session with one of the project's containers
26. **start**: starts a project's containers
27. **stop**: stops (*and removes*) a project's containers
28. **version**: displays the version of DDEV installed
29. **xdebug**: enable, disable, or view the status of Xdebug in the *web* container

WHAT'S NEXT?

Now that you have an understanding of the basics of DDEV-Local, it's time to dig in further.

In the next chapter, we're going to use DDEV-Local commands for the first time. I'm going to show you how to install DDEV-Local on your machine. I've included instructions for Mac, Windows and Linux users.

CHAPTER 3.

PROFESSIONAL DEVELOPMENT WORKFLOWS EXPLAINED

In the previous chapter, I defined the problem and solution we're tackling in this book. Web projects are becoming more complex and so are the development tools we use.

In this chapter, let's explore what a modern development workflow should look like, and how DDEV-Local can help.

WHAT IS A PROFESSIONAL DEVELOPMENT WORKFLOW?

In my experience, a modern development workflow often has these characteristics:

1. Multiple developers, each with their own local development environment.
2. A remote development (*dev*) environment where the development team can share their work.
3. A remote testing (*test*) environment for quality assurance team members to do their work.
4. A remote production (*live*) environment.
5. All environments using a single remote Git repository for

the project's codebase.

6. Optionally, you can have additional remote development environments for each branch of the code repository.

7. While some projects include continuous integration/continuous deployment (*CI/CD*) functionality, for the sake of this discussion, let's set CI/CD to the side for now.

I also find that many projects follow these three "best practice" rules:

1. Developers only add code to the repository from a local development environment. They do not modify code in any remote environment.

2. Once developers add new code to the repository, it must go through dev and test environments before they add it to the live environment. You want to properly vet and test the new code before adding it to the live environment.

3. The database and content files on the production environment are canonical and shall never be overwritten.

These rules ensure that developers properly test all code prior to deploying the code in the production environment. They also make sure that the developers never overwrite the production environment's data.

In this next image, I've illustrated a basic professional development workflow. While all environments can pull from the remote Git repository, only local environments can push code to it. Also, the project database is never moved *up* from local to dev/test/live – it is always moved *down*. This image exemplifies a "code flows up, data flows down" development workflow strategy.

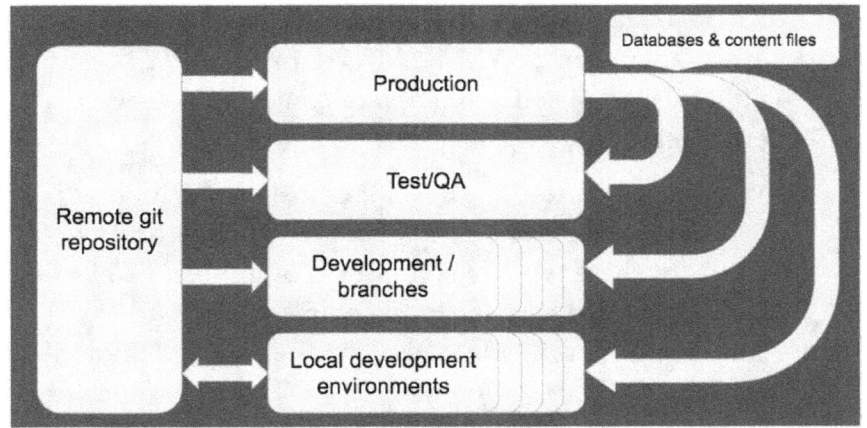

> The databases and content files can also be moved *down* from dev and test to local. However, this was not included in the diagram for clarity.

WHY ARE DEVELOPMENT WORKFLOWS DIFFICULT TO MANAGE?

Now we have a clear understanding of what our development workflows *should* look like. Why is it often so difficult to follow these best practices?

The problem lies in how we configure our environments. Each environment's configuration includes all the software and tools required to build, test, and serve the project.

Here are some ways that you can configure local environments:

1. **Native**: The developer installs and configures each tool independently and globally on their local machine. This results in all projects on the machine using the same tools and versions. This is often time-consuming and inflexible.

2. **All-in-one**: The developer installs the tools as a single executable, such as WAMP, MAMP or XAMPP. These are often easy to install, but not very configurable nor extendable.
3. **Virtual machines**: The developer installs the tools as part of a virtual machine on their computer. The learning curve for these types of solutions is often steep. You can customize and share the local environment, but sometimes it's difficult to get it configured and up-and-running.
4. **Docker-based (custom)**: Using native Docker commands and tools, the developer can customize a local development environment on a per-project bases. However, you will need a strong knowledge of Docker and Docker Compose.
5. **Docker-based (abstracted)**: A wrapper tool abstracts the standard Docker and Docker Compose commands to provide a much simpler way of creating and managing a Docker-based local development environment. This is what DDEV-Local does.

Unfortunately, on many situations, it's up to each developer to set up their own environment. If you're working in a team, there is no guarantee that all team members have configured their environments the same way, which will lead to issues.

1. Bugs can appear in one environment but not in another.
2. Tests that pass in one environment may not pass in other environments.
3. Performance tuning in one environment may not result in similar improvements in other environments.

If each developer is responsible for configuring their own local environment, you may end up with a situation like the image below. This is a root cause of the "it works on my machine" type of bug.

| Production |
| Test/QA |
| Development / branches |

Local dev environment 1	Mac OS X PHP 5.3 Apache Git MariaDB Composer	
Local dev environment 2	Windows PHP 7.1 Gulp NGINX Git Bower MySql Composer	
Local dev environment 3	Mac OS X PHP 7.2 NGINX Git Behat MySql Composer	

Clearly, there is a big advantage to simplifying the setup of a local development environment for each project and being able to share the setup configuration among team members. This is one of the reasons why I recommend using DDEV-Local. You can use DDEV-Local to create reliable, flexible and shareable environments. If your team members are using the same environment, the project will have fewer bugs and a better, more professional, development workflow.

WHAT'S NEXT?

In this chapter, we talked about what's required for a modern local development environment and why it's so important.

Let's be clear about our goals for a modern local development environment:

1. It should be easy and quick to install.
2. Each project should have its own flexible configuration.

3. Each project should have the same environment configuration for all team members.
4. It should be easy-to-learn and use local environment management tools.
5. It should allow users to get up-and-running on a project quickly.
6. It should integrate with modern hosting platforms.

The following chapters of this book will demonstrate how DDEV-Local achieves each of the items on the wish list. Along the way, we'll dive deeper into some areas with step-by-step examples of how to leverage this powerful tool. At the end of this process, you'll have a modern local development tool that is flexible, easy-to-use, quick to set up, and one that allows your projects and entire development team to work more efficiently.

Turn the page, and let's start exploring the basics of DDEV-Local.

CHAPTER 4.

INSTALLING DDEV-LOCAL EXPLAINED

This chapter is divided into different sections, one for each operating system: Mac, Windows, and Linux.

In each section, I'll give you a single recommended installation process. Other installation methods are available at:

> https://ddev.readthedocs.io/en/latest/

First, follow the installation instructions for your machine. Then, go to the section called, "Confirming Your Installation Explained". If you can successfully run the three commands, you've installed DDEV-Local and are ready to move on to the next chapter.

HOW TO INSTALL DDEV-LOCAL ON MAC

There are several prerequisites to install and run DDEV-Local on a Mac. You will need OS X Mojave (*version 10.14*) or a more recent version.

First, you'll need the **Xcode command line tools**. Apple provides a set of command-line tools that are helpful with development via the command-line. The Homebrew package manager requires some of the tools included in this set.

- **use** `xcode-select --install` via the command-line (*using the "Terminal" app*) to install

Second, you'll need the "Homebrew package manager". *Homebrew* is an open-source "package manager" for Mac OS X. A package manager is an application that helps to download and install "packages" of (*usually open-source*) software. Packages often depend on specific versions of other packages, and keeping track of the various dependencies and installation processes is often tedious. A package manager handles all this for us. **Installation** instructions are available on the Homebrew home at `https://brew.sh`.

Finally, you'll need *Docker for Mac*. Docker is the primary underlying technology of DDEV-Local. It is Docker that allows DDEV-Local to create and manage "containers" for each of your projects. In addition, Docker for Mac includes Docker Composer, a tool for managing sets of containers. Docker provides a free *Docker Community Edition for Mac*, which you can **download** and **install** from `https://store.docker.com/editions/community/docker-ce-desktop-mac`.

Once you have the prerequisites installed, you're ready to install DDEV-Local. '

- **run** the installation by using the following command and responding to any prompts

```
brew tap drud/ddev && brew install ddev
```

HOW TO INSTALL DDEV-LOCAL ON WINDOWS

This section focuses on installing DDEV-Local on Windows 10 Home, Pro, and Enterprise using WSL 2 (*Windows Subsystem for Linux*). This is the recommended method for installing

DDEV-Local on Windows. WSL 2 is a Microsoft-supported method of running Linux in a Windows environment. The instructions provided by the DDEV-Local team include installing WSL 2 and the Ubuntu Linux distribution (*"distro"*) and then installing DDEV-Local in Ubuntu. The end result is much more performant than installing DDEV-Local directly on Windows.

One downside of using WSL 2 is the fact that it is not recommended to share the project directory with both the Ubuntu file system and the Windows file system. While it is possible, it has a negative effect on performance. Instead it is recommended to use Microsoft's Visual Studio Code (*often referred to as "VS Code"*) and the "Remote Development extension pack" to access the Ubuntu file system from Windows. Instructions for this are included below.

If you'd prefer to NOT install DDEV-Local on Windows using WSL 2, there are legacy installation instructions available at

```
https://ddev.readthedocs.io/en/stable/#installation
```

The process for installing WSL 2 and DDEV-Local can be quite detailed depending on whether or not you have WSL 2 installed yet and other factors. The DDEV-Local team has put together some excellent instructions and resources for installation, and rather than repeating them here, it is best to just link to them directly, as they are updated periodically.

We recommend the following process:

1. **Review** the instructions at `https://ddev.readthedocs.io/en/stable/#installation`
2. **Watch** the screencast at `https://www.ddev.com/ddev-local/watch-ddev-local-from-scratch-with-windows-wsl2/`

3. **Perform** the necessary steps on your system.

Some additional installation notes as I went through the process on a Windows 10 Pro machine that did NOT have WSL 2 previously installed:

- **use** `ddev export-db` to backup any local databases you want to keep
- **ensure** that Docker for Windows is up-to-date
- **access** the administrative PowerShell via the Windows Start Menu
    - **search** for "Windows PowerShell"
    - **click** to "Run as Administrator"

The instructions provided by the DDEV-Local team mainly use the PowerShell command line.

- **use** `choco upgrade chocolatey` to ensure Chocolatey is installed (`https://docs.chocolatey.org/en-us/choco/setup`) and up-to-date

After installing a WSL2 distro (*Ubuntu*),

- **click** the "Launch" button to complete installation of the distro
- **use** `wsl -l -v` to confirm that the proper distro is the default (*if it isn't, use* `wsl --setdefault=Ubuntu` *to set the default*)

Once the Ubuntu distro is up-and-running, interact with it via its command line, NOT PowerShell (*accessible from the Windows Start Menu as "Ubuntu"*) . For example, to confirm that `mkcert` is working with Ubuntu,

- **run** `echo $CAROOT` from the Ubuntu command line

IF `docker ps` from the Ubuntu command line returns a permission denied error, **restart** Docker for Windows. Within the Ubuntu command line, you may need to use the right-click to **paste** the contents of your clipboard.

- **use** `brew install gcc && brew tap drud/ddev && brew install ddev` to complete DDEV -Local installation
- **use** `ddev version` to confirm installation

If no version is returned, try re-running the installation command.

Separate installation of Git is NOT necessary because it is included with the Ubuntu distro.

Installing VSCode and accessing your DDEV-Local projects

The recommended IDE for working with DDEV-Local project on WSL 2 is Visual Studio Code (*VS Code*). Traditional, Windows-based IDEs are less than ideal because the codebase for DDEV-Local projects on WSL 2 lives in the Ubuntu virutal machine. Without sharing the project directory with the Windows File System (*WFS*), it is not available to Windows applications. While sharing the project directly between the Ubuntu VM and WFS is fairly comment, it is not very performant.

Luckily, VS Code has a "Remote Development extension" that integrates natively with the Ubuntu VM – thus removing the need for sharing the directory between operating systems. Use the instructions on `https://code.visualstudio.com/docs/remote/wsl` to get started.

Some additional installation notes as I went through the process on a Windows 10 Pro machine that did NOT have VS Code previously installed:

After downloading and starting the installer,

- **keep** the "Add to path" option selected (*should be preselected on the "Select Additional Tasks" page*)

Once installed,

- **open** VS Code
- **install** recommended extensions for use with WSL 2. (*you'll likely have a notification in the lower-right-hand corner prompting you to do this*)
- **ignore** the "Install the Remote Development extension pack" step in the documentation

From the VS Code "Terminal" menu,

- **select** "New Terminal" (*this opens a new PowerShell terminal interface*)
- **use** the `wsl` command in PowerShell to connect to your default distro (*Ubuntu*)
- **use** `cd ~` to navigate to the home directory in Ubuntu

From here, you can use DDEV-Local commands! If this is your first time using DDEV-Local in WSL 2, then it is suggested to,

- **create** a new "sites" directory in your home directory

You can create your first DDEV-Local site within the new "sites" directory one of two ways:

1. cloning an existing project
2. using the `ddev composer create` command to start a new one

To open the codebase in VS Code for the current project (*as defined by your location on the command line*),

- **use** the `code` command from the project root

This will trigger a one-time tool download followed by a new VS Code window with your project directory open and ready for coding!

> The combination of WSL 2, DDEV-Local, and VS Code is a major improvement for working with PHP-based projects in Windows. Once up-and-running, its performance and access to Windows-based tools makes it once again a worthy alternative to other operating system's development environments.

HOW TO INSTALL DDEV-LOCAL ON LINUX

This section will summarize the installation of DDEV-Local on Linux. The instructions may vary depending on the exact flavor and version of Linux that you are using.

In order to install DDEV-Local on Linux, there are several prerequisites:

First, you will need *Docker*. I recommend installing Docker using the "Install using the repository" method for your particular flavor of Linux. These links have installation instructions for three popular flavors of Linux:

1. Debian: `https://docs.docker.com/install/linux/docker-ce/debian/`
2. Fedora: `https://docs.docker.com/install/linux/docker-ce/fedora/`
3. Ubuntu: `https://docs.docker.com/install/linux/docker-ce/ubuntu/`

Pay close attention to the instructions for your version of Linux, as the instructions may have subtle but important differences. For example, at the time of this writing, to install Docker on Ubuntu 18.04, you need to add the *edge* repository in addition to the *stable* repository in the following command:

```
sudo add-apt-repository "deb [arch=amd64] https://download.docker.com/linux/ubuntu $(lsb_release -cs) stable edge"
```

Second, you need *Docker Compose*, which is a tool for managing sets of containers. The official documentation has instructions for installing Docker Compose on Linux at https://docs.docker.com/compose/install/.

Third, I recommend you complete these post-installation steps for Docker and Docker Compose: https://docs.docker.com/install/linux/linux-postinstall/.

Finally, you should start running Docker. To **run** Docker from the command-line, use the following command:

```
sudo service docker start
```

The recommended way to install DDEV-Local on Linux is via Linuxbrew (http://linuxbrew.sh/), the Homebrew package manager for Linux. With Linuxbrew installed, DDEV-Local can be installed with the following:

```
brew tap drud/ddev && brew install ddev
```

CONFIRMING YOUR INSTALLATION

Whether you're on Mac, Windows or Linux, once installation is complete, it's time to confirm that DDEV-Local is ready to use.

- **use** `which ddev` to verify that DDEV-Local is accessible

This command should return the path to the ddev executable.

On Windows, depending on your console emulator, you may have to use `where ddev`.

- **use** `ddev version` to confirm the version of DDEV-Local that was just installed
- **use** `ddev help` to review a list of the available DDEV-Local commands

If these three commands each return reasonable results, you have successfully installed DDEV-Local.

WHAT'S NEXT?

In the next chapter, we'll take advantage of our newly-installed DDEV-Local and spin up a new Drupal 8 web site project.

DDEV-LOCAL COMMAND OVERVIEW

Below is a list of DDEV-Local commands we have covered:

1. `help`
2. `version`

CHAPTER 5.

INSTALLING A NEW DRUPAL SITE IN DDEV-LOCAL EXPLAINED

In the previous chapter, I showed you how to install DDEV-Local.

In this chapter, I'll show you how to install a blank, new Drupal 9 site. You can use this to start a fresh project, or you can simply use it as a development playground.

Starting with Drupal 9, the Drupal community has been slowly adopting Composer (https://getcomposer.org/) as the de-facto way of managing a Drupal project codebase. With the release of Drupal 8.8, the community now provides an official Composer template:

> https://www.drupal.org/docs/develop/using-composer/starting-a-site-using-drupal-composer-project-templates

Prior to Drupal 8.8, the best practice for creating a new Drupal 8 site was to use the Drupal Composer/Drupal Project template: https://github.com/drupal-composer/drupal-project/.

In this chapter, I'm going to show you how to create a new Drupal 9 project using both methods along with the following assumptions:

1. Project dependencies will not be committed to the local Git repository.
2. Composer is NOT installed on the host operating system. We will see how to utilize the version of Composer that is installed in the DDEV-Local *web* container. This will require us to create the DDEV-Local project containers prior to creating the codebase, as we will need Composer to create the codebase.

> DDEV-Local 1.16.0 introduced support for Composer 2, but Composer 1 is still used by default in DDEV-Local. To utilize Composer 2, **use** `ddev config --composer-version=2` to change the `composer_version` value in your project's ".ddev/config.yaml file" to 2.

STEP #1. CREATE THE CODEBASE

In this first step, we will create the DDEV-Local containers for this project and use Composer to create the Drupal 9 codebase.

- **navigate** from the command line to your local "Sites" directory (*create directory first if necessary*)
- **use** `mkdir myproject` to create a new, empty, project directory

In this command, `myproject` is a short, machine-name type name for your project. This is often all lower-case and should not include any non-alphanumeric characters.

- **use** `cd myproject` to navigate from the command line into the new project directory
- **run** the command below from the command line

```
ddev config --project-name myproject --docroot web
--create-docroot --project-type drupal9
```

This is an alternate way of running the "ddev config" command that passes in the information necessary to configure the default DDEV-Local containers. This will result in a ".ddev" directory in your project ("myproject") directory. This directory will contain the DDEV-Local configuration information for this project.

- **run** `ddev start` from the command line to create the containers for this project
- **use** the following `ddev composer create` command to install the codebase using the official Drupal community Composer template (*use this method ONLY for Drupal 8.8 or later*

```
ddev composer create drupal/recommended-project
--no-interaction
```

- **confirm** that it is okay to overwrite everything in the project directory ("myproject", *in this example. It is okay to respond "yes"*)

The `ddev composer create` command is basically a wrapper around "composer create-project" that is designed to work within the context of DDEV containers.

> **Note**: DDEV knows to install the project in the current directory, so we do NOT need to pass in the name of the directory to install the project in.

The result of this command is the Drupal 9 codebase installed in the "myproject" directory. By using the `ddev composer` command, you are using the version of Composer that in installed in the default DDEV-Local *web* container (*not any version of Composer installed on your host operating system.*)

> We are unable to use the `composer create-project` command to create the codebase directly in the "myproject" directory, because Composer requires the directory to be empty, and the `.ddev` directory is already present. The `ddev composer create` command sidesteps this issue.

The `ddev composer create` command does several things:

1. It downloads the project from the source repository (*GitHub, in this case*).
2. It automatically runs `composer install` to download all dependencies and run any pre- and post-install Composer scripts, as specified in the "composer.json" file provided by the template.

The `ddev composer` command can be used to run other Composer commands during the lifecycle of a project, including update, require, and remove.

If you're interested in using the Drupal Composer/Drupal Project template (`https://github.com/drupal-composer/drupal-project/`) for versions of Drupal core 8.7 and earlier, then instead of the previous command, you would use the following: (*this command uses most of the default parameters listed in the Drupal Composer/Drupal Project template's installation instructions, but with a few minor changes*).

```
ddev composer create drupal-composer/drupal-project:8.x-dev
--stability dev --no-interaction
```

While the Drupal Composer/Drupal Project template works for versions of Drupal core greater than 8.7, it is the recommended best practice to use the official Drupal community Composer template used above.

At this point, the codebase is just about ready for use.

STEP #2. CONFIGURE THE DRUPAL SETTINGS FILES

With a Drupal 9 codebase now present, we can configure the Drupal 9 settings files with best practices in mind.

First, let's make sure we're using a copy of Drupal 9's "default.settings.php" file as the base for our "settings.php" file. In the initial `ddev config` step above, while DDEV-Local created a new "settings.php" file for us, best practice dictates that it should be based on "default.settings.php":

```
cp web/sites/default/default.settings.php web/sites/default/settings.php
```

It is a good practice to utilize the core Drupal 9 "web/sites/example.settings.local.php" file.

- **run** the following command to copy and rename the file for use

```
cp web/sites/example.settings.local.php web/sites/default/settings.local.php
```

- **edit** the "settings.php" file and **uncomment** the following lines near the bottom of the file

```
if (file_exists($app_root . '/' . $site_path . '/settings.local.php')) {
```

```
include $app_root . '/' . $site_path .
'/settings.local.php';
}
```

Because we created a new "settings.php" above, we need to have DDEV-Local re-add the conditional include for "settings.ddev.php".

- **run** `ddev restart` to restart the project's containers
- **use** `ddev describe` once restarted to be reminded of the project's local URLs
- **navigate** to one of the project's URLs (*try using the* `ddev launch` *command! where you should be greeted with the Drupal 9 installer page*)

As you go through the installer, you'll notice that you will **skip** the "Set up database" step, as DDEV-Local's creation of the "settings.ddev.php" file already took care of this for you!

AN ALTERNATIVE METHOD TO INSTALL A NEW SITE

This chapter assumes Composer isn't installed on the host operating system. This requires us to use the version of Composer that is installed in the default DDEV-Local *web* container. However, if Composer is installed on your operating system, then *Step #1. Creating the Codebase* section becomes much simpler.

> This method should only be used if the minor version of PHP on your host operating system is the same as the what is configured for use in your DDEV web container.

- **navigate** into your "Sites" directory
- **run** the following command to create the codebase

```
composer create-project drupal/recommended-project myproject --no-interaction
```

In this case, replace `myproject` with a short, machine-name for your project. This will be similar to naming the project directory earlier in this chapter.

That's it! At this point, your codebase is ready for *Step #2. Configure the Containers and the Drupal Settings Files.*

WHAT'S NEXT?

In this chapter, you've seen how to install a new Drupal 9 site in DDEV-Local.

In the next chapter, we'll learn how to spin up a new WordPress 5 web site project locally using DDEV-Local.

DDEV-LOCAL COMMAND OVERVIEW

Below is a list of DDEV-Local commands we have covered:

1. help
2. version
3. composer
4. config
5. describe
6. launch
7. restart
8. start

CHAPTER 6.

INSTALLING A NEW WORDPRESS SITE IN DDEV-LOCAL EXPLAINED

In the previous chapter, I showed you how to get a new Drupal 8 site up-and-running on your local machine using DDEV-Local.

In this chapter, I'll show you how to install a blank, new WordPress site using two different methods. First, I'll demonstrate how to get a new WordPress site up-and-running locally by simply downloading the codebase from `WordPress.org`.

In the second example, we'll walk through how to utilize Bedrock (`https://roots.io/bedrock/`), a Composer-based template for creating a WordPress project codebase.

EXAMPLE #1. CODEBASE DOWNLOADED FROM WORDPRESS.ORG

The traditional way of creating a new WordPress site in a local environment is to download the WordPress codebase from wordpress.org.

- **click** "Get WordPress" button to download the latest version of WordPress (*As of the writing of this chapter, the current version of WordPress was 5.0.1.*)

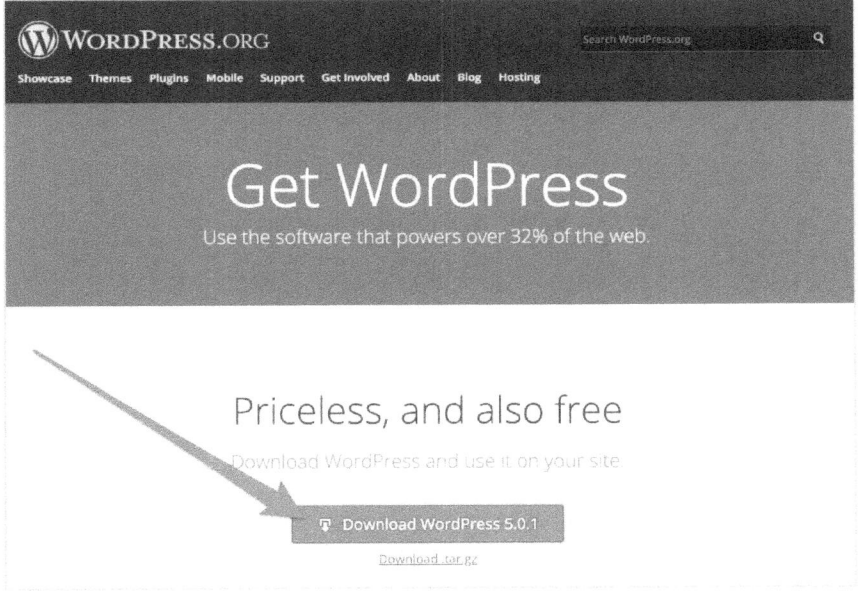

- **click** "Download WordPress 5.0.1 button
- **extract** the compressed directory once downloaded
- **move** it into your local "Sites" directory (*or wherever you'd like your new WordPress project to reside on your local hard drive*).

In this example, I'm navigating into my "sites" directory, then extracting the downloaded file from my "~/Downloads/" directory and moving it to my "~/sites/" directory via the command line:

```
$ cd sites
$ unzip ~/Downloads/wordpress.zip
```

This results in the WordPress codebase in a "sites/wordpress/" directory.

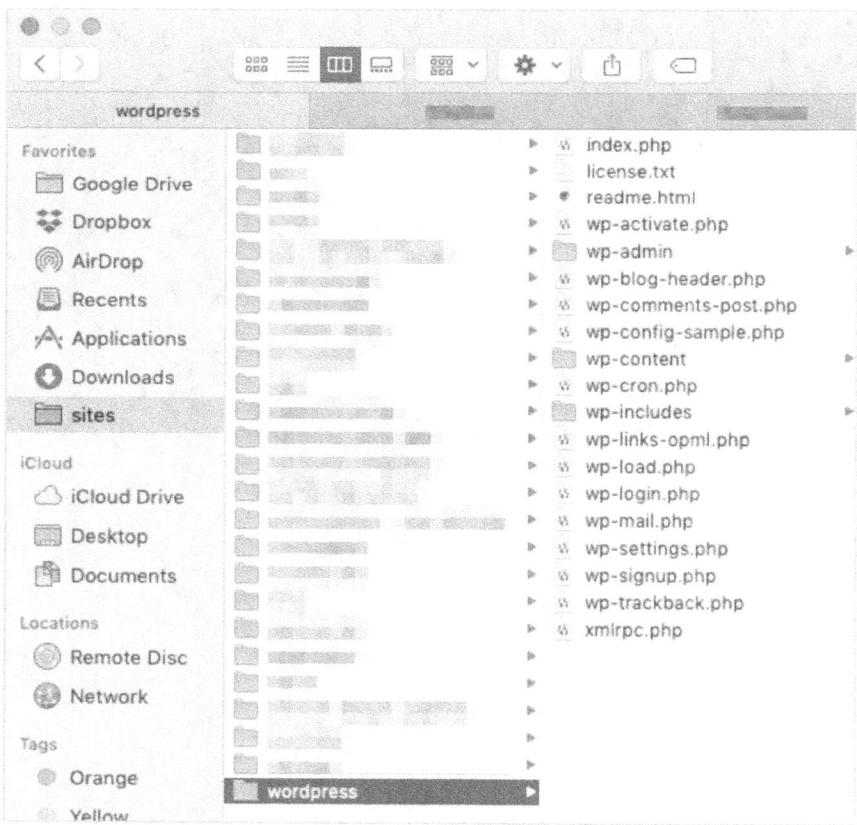

> An alternative, more command-line friendly way of getting a standard WordPress codebase is to use:
>
> wget http://wordpress.org/latest.tar.gz
>
> This will download the latest version of WordPress to the current directory. Once complete, use the following command to extract the archive into a directory named "wordpress":
>
> tar xvf latest.tar.gz

- **rename** the project directory from "wordpress" to "ddevwordpress"

It is considered a best practice to rename the project directory to the name of the project. Again, I'll make this change via the command line using the mv (*move*) command, then navigate to inside the project directory:

```
$mv wordpress ddevwordpress
$ccd ddevwordpress
```

- **configure** a set of DDEV-Local containers for the project.

We'll use the ddev config command to answer a few questions about the project so that DDEV-Local can make some assumptions about the configuration of the project's containers.

```
$ ddev config
Creating a new ddev project config in the current directory
(/Users/michael/sites/ddevwordpress)
Once completed, your configuration will be written to
/Users/michael/sites/ddevwordpress/.ddev/config.yaml

Project name (ddevwordpress):
```

```
The docroot is the directory from which your site is
served. This is a relative path from your project root
(/Users/michael/sites/ddevwordpress)
You may leave this value blank if your site files are in
the project root
Docroot Location (current directory):
Found a wordpress codebase at /Users/michael/sites/
ddevwordpress.
Project Type [drupal8, wordpress, typo3, backdrop, php,
drupal6, drupal7] (wordpress):
Configuration complete. You may now run 'ddev start'.
```

This will result in a ".ddev" directory in your project (*"ddevwordpress"*) directory. This directory will contain the DDEV-Local configuration information for this project.

> **Note**: I didn't actually need to answer any of the questions that the `ddev config` command prompted me for – it actually already knew the answers! DDEV-Local sniffed around the project directory and correctly guessed the project name (`ddevwordpress`), the location of the docroot (*the current, "ddevwordpress", directory*), and the project type (`wordpress`).

The `ddev config` command actually did one additional thing for us – it automatically created some very useful files for our local environment:

1. The "/wp-config.php" file – this standard WordPress file typically contains important variables for the site, including security hashes, database connection information, and environment variables. DDEV-Local creates this file, populates it with the necessary information, and adds a conditional include to a "/wp-config-ddev.php" file. As DDEV-Local generated this file,

it is recommended that developers do not make any additional changes to this file, as DDEV-Local may regenerate it in a future update.

2. The "/wp-config-ddev.php" file – this file contains the local database connection, the local URL, and enables WordPress's debugging in the DDEV-Local environment. This file should not be modified manually, as DDEV-Local may regenerate it in a future update. Nor should this file should be committed to the project's Git repository. It is automatically included in the ".gitignore" file created by the `ddev config` command.

3. The "/.gitignore" file – this file contains an entry for the "/wp-config-ddev.php" file so that it is not added to the project's Git repository.

- **run** $ `ddev start` from the command line to create the containers for this project

As this is a new project, you'll likely be prompted to enter in your computer's password (*actually, the password for the user account you're logged into your computer with*) in order for DDEV-Local to modify your local *hosts* file with the new local URL to access the project locally.

```
$ ddev start
Starting ddevwordpress...
ddev needs to add an entry to your hostfile.
It will require administrative privileges via the sudo
command, so you may be required to enter your password for
sudo. ddev is about to issue the command:
sudo /usr/local/bin/ddev hostname ddevwordpress.ddev.site
127.0.0.1
Please enter your password if prompted.
Running Command Command=sudo /usr/local/bin/ddev hostname
ddevwordpress.ddev.site 127.0.0.1
Password:
Creating volume "ddevwordpress-mariadb" with default driver
```

```
Creating ddev-ddevwordpress-db ... done
Creating ddev-ddevwordpress-dba ... done
Creating ddev-ddevwordpress-web ... done

Network ddev_default is external, skipping
Creating ddev-router ... done

Successfully started ddevwordpress
Project can be reached at http://ddevwordpress.ddev.site,
https://ddevwordpress.ddev.site, http://127.0.0.1:32814
```

At this point, you should be able to go to the local URL provided by DDEV-Local and view the WordPress installation screen.

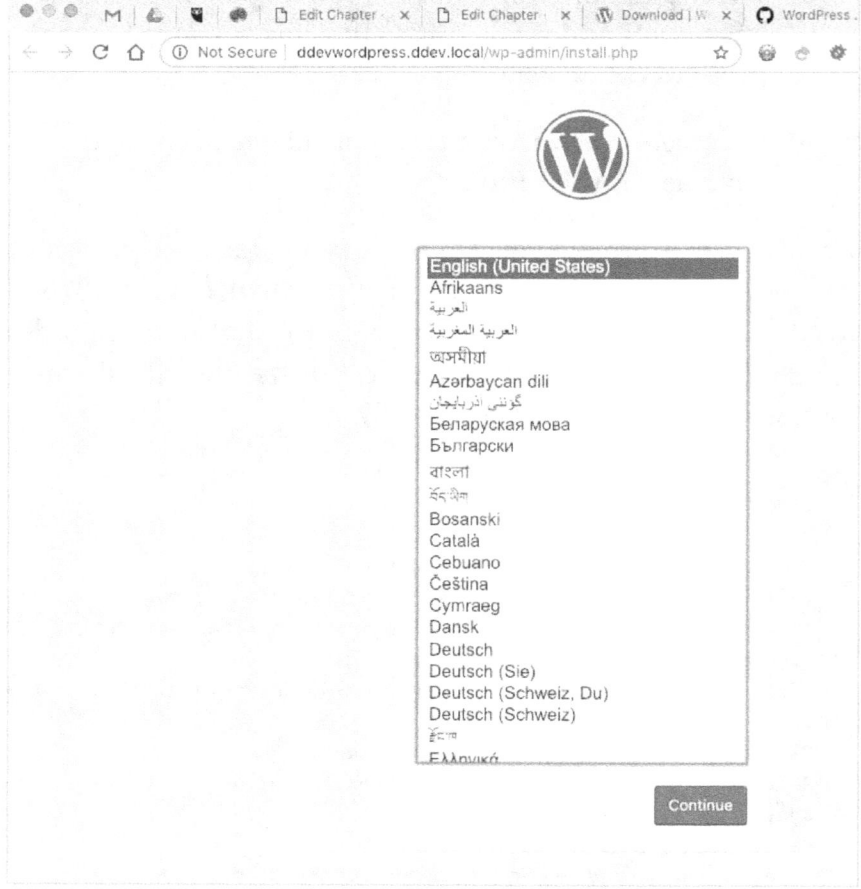

As you step through the installation steps in your browser, note that you will not have to enter the database connection information for this local install. This is because during the ddev config process, DDEV-Local created the "/wp-config-ddev.php" file pre-populated with the database connection information – handy!

Once the installation steps are complete, you should be ready to work with your new local WordPress site! You can interact with your local site just like you would interact with it if it was hosted remotely. This includes installing plugins from the dashboard and all other admin functionality.

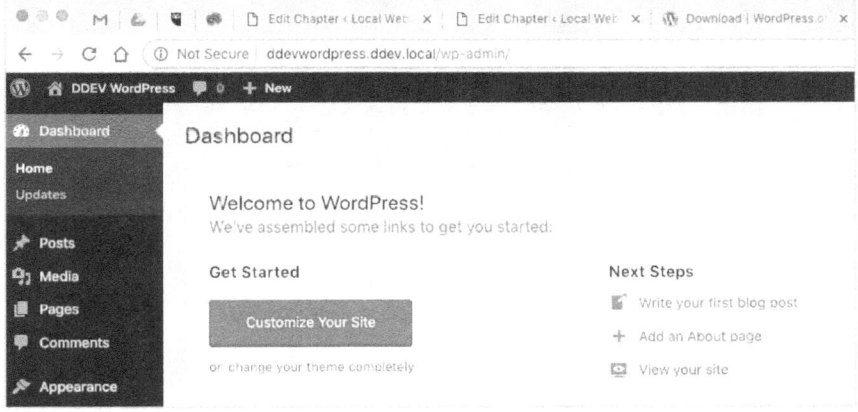

EXAMPLE #2. CODEBASE CREATED WITH BEDROCK

Bedrock (https://roots.io/bedrock/) is a modern, Composer-based boilerplate for
assembling and managing a WordPress codebase. For developers who want to adopt modern PHP practices, using Bedrock for your WordPress projects is an excellent first step. Bedrock provides several best-practice focused advantages:

1. The use of Composer to manage project dependencies – without project dependencies being committed to the

project repository.

2. The placement of the document root inside a directory in the project root – a "nested docroot".

3. An updated organization of WordPress files inside the document root designed to provide better code organization – separating WordPress core files from third-party plugins and themes and renaming the "wp-content" directory to "app".

4. A dedicated "config" directory on the project root to manage configurations for various project environments utilizing the Dotenv (`https://www.npmjs.com/package/dotenv`) project.

5. More secure passwords via the "wp-password-bcrypt" plugin (`https://github.com/roots/wp-password-bcrypt`).

In this example, I'm going to show you how to create a new, Bedrock-based WordPress 5 project with the assumption that Composer is NOT installed on the host operating system. We will see how to utilize the version of Composer that is installed in the DDEV-Local *web* container. This will require us to create the DDEV-Local project containers prior to creating the codebase, as we will need Composer to create the codebase.

Step #1. Get the Bedrock-based WordPress codebase

First you need to create the DDEV-Local containers for this project. Then you'll need to use Composer to create the Bedrock-based WordPress codebase.

- **navigate** from the command line to your local "Sites" directory

- **use** `$ mkdir ddevbedrock` to create a new, empty, project directory

In this example, I'm going to use `ddevbedrock` as the short, machine-name type name for this project directory. The project directory is typically all lower-case and should not include any non-alphanumeric characters.

- **use** $ `cd ddevbedrock` to navigate from the command line into the new project directory

At this point in time, we do not yet have the codebase – this is because we need to run a Composer command to get the codebase, and this example is assuming that we do not have Composer installed on our local operating system. Thus we will have to use the version of Composer that is included in the DDEV-Local web container.

So, we will:

1. Set up a generic set of DDEV-Local containers for this project.
2. Run the Composer command to get the codebase.
3. Reconfigure the DDEV-Local containers with the new codebase.

- **run** the following `ddev config` command from the command line (*and accept all default values*) to configure the initial set of DDEV-Local containers for this project

```
$ ddev config
Creating a new ddev project config in the current directory
(/Users/michael/sites/ddevbedrock) Once completed, your
configuration will be written to /Users/michael/sites/
ddevbedrock/.ddev/config.yaml

Project name (ddevbedrock):

The docroot is the directory from which your site is
served. This is a relative path from your project root
(/Users/michael/sites/ddevbedrock) You may leave this value
```

```
blank if your site files are in the project root Docroot
Location (current directory): Found a php codebase at
/Users/michael/sites/ddevbedrock.
Project Type [wordpress, typo3, backdrop, php, drupal6,
drupal7, drupal8] (php): Project type has no settings paths
configured, so not creating settings file. Configuration
complete. You may now run 'ddev start'.
```

Notice that the current project type is "php". This is because we do not have the codebase yet. Running the `ddev config` command will result in a ".ddev" directory in your project directory. This directory will contain the DDEV-Local configuration information for this project.

- **run** `$ ddev start` from the command line to create the initial containers for this project

Again, you'll likely have to enter in your host operating system user account password in order to add the necessary entries to your *hosts* file.

Now that we have a set of DDEV-Local containers up-and-running, we can utilize the `ddev composer` command to create our Bedrock-based WordPress codebase. The official documentation for the Bedrock project has the Composer command to create a new Bedrock project as `composer create-project roots/bedrock`, but we are going to use the `ddev composer create` command instead.

This is a DDEV-Local wrapper around the `composer create-project` command designed to allow you to create a Composer project inside of a DDEV-Local *web* container while utilizing the version of Composer that comes automatically with a DDEV-Local *web* container.

```
$ ddev composer create roots/bedrock
Warning: Any existing contents of the project root (/Users/
michael/sites/ddevbedrock) will be removed
Would you like to continue? [Y/n] (yes):
Removing any existing files in project root
Executing composer command: composer create-project roots/
bedrock /var/www/html/.tmp_nKwjhg

Installing roots/bedrock (1.10.1)
 - Installing roots/bedrock (1.10.1): Downloading (100%)
Created project in /var/www/html/.tmp_nKwjhg
> php -r "copy('.env.example', '.env');"
Loading composer repositories with package information
Installing dependencies (including require-dev) from lock
file
Package operations: 9 installs, 0 updates, 0 removals
 - Installing roots/wordpress-core-installer (1.1.0):
Downloading (100%)
 - Installing composer/installers (v1.6.0): Loading from
cache
 - Installing oscarotero/env (v1.1.0): Downloading (100%)
 - Installing roots/wordpress (5.0.1): Downloading (100%)
 - Installing roots/wp-config (1.0.0): Downloading (100%)
 - Installing roots/wp-password-bcrypt (1.0.0): Downloading
(100%)
 - Installing vlucas/phpdotenv (v2.5.1): Loading from cache
 - Installing squizlabs/php_codesniffer (3.3.2): Loading
from cache
Generating autoload files
Moving installation to project root
Removing temporary install directory
```

This command actually creates the project in a temporary directory first, then moves it into the project root directory. This is because `composer create-project` requires the target directory of the create-project command to be completely empty. But, the presence of the ".ddev/" directory violates this.

So, in effect, the `ddev composer create` command sidesteps this requirement by first creating the project in a new, empty temporary directory before moving it into the main project directory.

The result of this command is the Bedrock-based WordPress codebase installed in your project directory.

Like the `composer create-project` command, the `ddev composer create` command does several things:

1. It downloads the project from the source repository (*GitHub, in this case*).

2. It automatically runs `composer install` to download all dependencies and run any pre- and post-install Composer scripts, as specified in the "composer.json" file provided by Bedrock.

You can use the `ddev composer` command to run other Composer commands during the lifecycle of a project, including update, require, and remove.

Step #2. Configure the local environment
With a Bedrock-based WordPress codebase now present,

- **rerun** the `ddev config` command as follows to update our local development environment's configuration for WordPress

```
$ ddev config --project-name ddevbedrock --docroot web
--project-type wordpress
```

This is an alternative way of running the `ddev config` command we saw earlier that passes in the required information via flags, rather than providing the same information via interactive prompts.

As of the writing of this chapter, the result of this command includes a warning that "An existing user-managed wp-config.php file has been detected!" As we saw in the previous example, DDEV-Local would normally create the "wp-config.php" file with the necessary information, but since Bedrock is already doing this, DDEV-Local takes a back seat and relinquishes control of the "wp-config.php" file to Bedrock.

As part of this command, DDEV-Local creates a "/web/wp-config-ddev.php" similar to the previous example, but we are NOT going to use it, as Bedrock utilizes the Dotenv project to manage environment configurations.

- **delete** "/web/wp-config-ddev.php" file

In order to complete the configuration process, we need to configure our local environment variables using the scaffolding that Dotenv (https://www.npmjs.com/package/dotenv) provides.

- **duplicate** the "/config/development.php" file to "/config/local.php" using the command line

```
$ cp config/environments/development.php config/environments/local.php
```

Dotenv allows for a configuration file for each environment. In this example, we're assuming the "development" environment is a shared development environment on a remote server, while the new "local" environment is our DDEV-local environment. While no changes are necessary in the new "/config/environments/local.php" file, it is here where debugging and other flags can be set for the local environment.

- **edit** the existing "/.env" file using the following command lines

This file, ignored by Git by default in Bedrock, contains environment-specific information for the project including the database connection information. This file is the reason that we do NOT need the DDEV-Local generated "/web/wp-config-ddev.php" that we deleted earlier.

```
DB_NAME=db
DB_USER=db
DB_PASSWORD=db

# Optional variables
DB_HOST=db
DB_PREFIX=wp_

WP_ENV=local
WP_HOME=http://ddevbedrock.ddev.site
WP_SITEURL=${WP_HOME}/wp

# Generate your keys here: https://roots.io/salts.html
AUTH_KEY='generateme'
SECURE_AUTH_KEY='generateme'
LOGGED_IN_KEY='generateme'
NONCE_KEY='generateme'
AUTH_SALT='generateme'
SECURE_AUTH_SALT='generateme'
LOGGED_IN_SALT='generateme'
NONCE_SALT='generateme'
```

Changes include:

1. The database name, user, password, and host are all "db" – these are default values for DDEV-Local databases.
2. The WP_HOME variable should be set to the URL of the local environment provided by DDEV-Local.

Because we made changes to the DDEV-Local project configuration above (*via the second* `ddev config` *command*),

- **run** `$ ddev restart` to restart the project's containers
- **navigate** to the project's URL you specified in the ".env" file

You should be greeted with the WordPress installer page!

WHAT'S NEXT?

In this chapter, you've seen how to install a new WordPress site in DDEV-Local using two different methods.

In the next chapter, I'll show you how to clone an existing Drupal 8 site to your local machine and get it up-and-running with DDEV-Local.

DDEV-LOCAL COMMAND OVERVIEW

Below is a list of DDEV-Local commands we have covered:

1. `help`
2. `version`
3. `composer`
4. `config`
5. `describe`
6. `launch`
7. `restart`
8. `start`

CHAPTER 7.

CLONING AN EXISTING DRUPAL SITE TO DDEV-LOCAL EXPLAINED

In a previous chapter, I showed you how to get a new Drupal 8 site up-and-running in DDEV-Local.

If the project already exists, then you'll want to clone the site from your project's remote repository. This allows you to get an up-to-date copy of the codebase, plus a complete history of the code changes. You will also need to get the site's database and content files in order to get the site up-and-running.

While DDEV-Local works with Drupal, TYPO3, WordPress, and other applications, in this chapter, we're going to clone a Drupal 8 site.

I've made a codebase, database, and content files directory available for you to practice with:

> https://github.com/ultimike/ddevdemo.

This codebase is configured so the Composer dependencies are committed to the repository. This means you will NOT need to run any Composer commands.

The database export is located in the "/db_export/" directory of the repository. The "files/" directory export is located in the "/files_export/" directory of the repository.

STEP #1. CLONE THE PROJECT

From your local command line, navigate to the directory where you want to clone the project to. Typically, this is your local "sites/" directory.

- **enter** the following command

```
git clone https://github.com/ultimike/ddevdemo.git
```

This will clone the entire project's history from GitHub to your computer, in a new directory named "ddevdemo". Once cloned, Git will create a working directory of the branch named "master". The general structure of the git clone command is:

```
git clone protocol://url_of_repository
name_of_local_directory_to_create
```

When you omit the "name_of_local_directory_to_create" parameter, the name of the directory is set to the name of the repository, in this case "ddevdemo".

After the git clone command is done, your local directory structure should look like this (*assuming you cloned into your "sites/" directory*):

```
- sites
  - ddevdemo
  - web/
  - (several other files and directories)
```

The *ddevdemo* site utilizes a *nested docroot,* meaning that Drupal is installed in the "web/" directory (the *docroot*) while the project root is in the "ddevdemo/" directory. The main advantage of utilizing a nested docroot is that anything not in the "web/" directory is normally not accessible via a web browser, as it is one-level "up" from the docroot. This is assuming a properly configured web server and that the site's domain name is pointing to the docroot.

This setup provides developers with a location to place files that are related to the project that should not be accessible via a URL. Some examples are configuration files, local development configuration, and automated tests.

The *ddevdemo* codebase is a Drupal 8 project that is based on the "drupal/recommended-project" Composer template: https://github.com/drupal/recommended-project. This is a best practice for organizing a Drupal 8, Composer-managed codebase. This Composer template provides the following features:

1. Nested docroot for the Drupal site ("/web").
2. "Above the docroot" directories for site configuration, drush, and other scripts.
3. A fully-Composer managed codebase (*including Drupal core being a dependency of the project*).
4. A robust Drupal core scaffolding plugin.

Once the site is successfully cloned,

- **use** cd ddevdemo to navigate into the project directory

STEP #2. LAUNCH THE DDEV-LOCAL CONTAINERS

The second step is to use DDEV-Local to get the site up-and-running on your local machine. Keep in mind that

DDEV-Local provides a set of Docker containers per project, so the containers will be configured specifically for this project.

- **run** `ddev config` from the command line

When you run this command without passing any parameters or flags, it will ask several questions so that it can provide a set of default Docker containers for the project. DDEV-Local will guess the correct answers based on the contents of the project directory; default values will be displayed in parentheses at the end of each question.

You can **respond** to DDEV-Local's questions with the following replies:

1. **Project name:** `ddevdemo` (*Typically, the project name is set as the same as the project directory name.*)

2. **Docroot location:** `web` (*As we're using the Drupal Composer/ Drupal Project template, this is the default location for the docroot. DDEV-Local will guess the proper value and provide it as an option in the prompt.*)

3. **Project type:** `drupal8` (*DDEV-Local will do its best to figure this out based on the codebase.*)

The entire output of the `ddev config` command should look similar to the following:

```
~/Sites/ddevdemo [master]$ ddev config

This will create a new ddev project config in the current
directory (/Users/michael/Sites/ddevdemo). Once completed,
your configuration will be written to:

/Users/michael/Sites/ddevdemo/.ddev/config.yaml

Project name (ddevdemo):
```

```
The docroot is the directory from which your site is
served. This is a relative path from
your project root (/Users/michael/Sites/ddevdemo)
You may leave this value blank if your site files are in
the project root
Docroot Location (web):
Found a drupal8 codebase at /Users/michael/Sites/ddevdemo/
web.
Project Type [wordpress, typo3, backdrop, php, drupal6,
drupal7, drupal8] (drupal8):
Ensuring write permissions for ddevdemo
Existing settings.php file does not include
settings.ddev.php, modifying to include
ddev settings
Configuration complete. You may now run 'ddev start'.
```

- **run** ddev start from the command line to download, create and run the containers for this project

You may have to enter your computer's password in order for DDEV-Local to add an entry to your hosts file for this project.

The entire output of this command should look similar to the following:

```
~/Sites/ddevdemo [master*]$ ddev start
Starting ddevdemo...
ddev needs to add an entry to your hostfile.
It will require administrative privileges via the sudo
command, so you may be required
to enter your password for sudo. ddev is about to issue the
command:

sudo /usr/local/bin/ddev hostname ddevdemo.ddev.site
127.0.0.1

Please enter your password if prompted.

Running Command Command=sudo /usr/local/bin/ddev hostname
ddevdemo.ddev.site 127.0.0.1
Creating ddev-ddevdemo-db ... done
```

```
Creating ddev-ddevdemo-dba ... done
Creating ddev-ddevdemo-web ... done
Network ddev_default is external, skipping
Creating ddev-router ... done
Ensuring write permissions for ddevdemo
Successfully started ddevdemo
Project can be reached at http://ddevdemo.ddev.site,
https://ddevcemo.ddev.site, http://127.0.0.1:32779
```

At this point, only the project's codebase is ready for you to use. Neither the database nor the "files/" directory is ready yet. Visiting one of the URLs provided by DDEV-Local will redirect you to Drupal 8's installation page. But, since this project includes a database, the next step is to import, not to install, and connect to the site's database.

STEP #3. IMPORT AND CONNECT TO THE DATABASE

Now that we have the complete codebase on our local environment with DDEV-Local up-and-running, the next step is to set up our local settings files and import the database.

- **set up** three settings files to manage general site settings, local settings, and DDEV-Local-specific settings:

1. ddevdemo/web/sites/default/settings.php (*This is the standard Drupal settings file and is typically part of the repository.*)

2. ddevdemo/web/sites/default/settings.ddev.php (*This contains the settings generated by the* ddev config *command and is not typically part of the repository.*)*This file includes the local database connection information. Git ignores this file via the "/ddevdemo/web/sites/default/.gitignore" file generated during the* ddev config *command.*)

3. ddevdemo/web/sites/default/settings.local.php (*This is a*

copy of the "ddevdemo/web/sites/example.settings.local.php" file, together with any additional local settings provided by the developer. This file is typically not part of the repository. Git ignores this file via this project's ".gitignore" file.)

With a Drupal 8 site, the "settings.ddev.php" file is automatically created during the `ddev config` process. You can modify the "settings.php" file with the addition of a conditional include of the "settings.ddev.php" file.

- **run** the following command from the project root in order to set up the "settings.local.php" file

```
cp web/sites/example.settings.local.php web/sites/default/settings.local.php
```

You can also use your operating system's GUI to **copy** and **rename** "web/sites/example.settings.local.php" to "`web/sites/default/settings.local.php`".

The "settings.php" file included with the codebase is already configured to conditionally include the "settings.local.php" file with the following code:

```
if (file_exists($app_root . '/' . $site_path . '/settings.local.php')) {
  include $app_root . '/' . $site_path . '/settings.local.php';
}
```

- **import** the database provided with this project (*in the "ddevdemo/db_backup/" directory*) with the following command

```
ddev import-db --src=db_backup/ddevdemo_db.sql
```

You will likely see a message confirming that the "settings.ddev.php" file is present and is being conditionally included in the "settings.php" file. This is normal.

> A common pitfall with this command occurs when a database dump file has an incorrect extension.
>
> For example: If a database dump file is provided that is compressed, but has the ".sql" extension, this command will fail. The Linux `file` command is helpful in determining the actual file type, regardless of the extension.
>
> ```
> $ file test.sql.gz
>   test.sql.gz: gzip compressed data, max compression, from Unix
> ```

At this point, if you visit one of the local site's URLs, your local copy of the DDEV Demo site should now load. However, you won't see any images yet.

STEP #4. PLACE THE CONTENT FILES

Now that we have the codebase and the database on our local environment with DDEV-Local up-and-running, it's time to import our content files. The DDEV Demo repository includes an archive of the necessary content files.

- **import** them into the site with the following `ddev import-files` command

```
ddev import-files --src=files_backup/ddevdemo_files.zip
```

This command will simply extract the archive and move it to

the proper location in the codebase, which is "/ddevdemo/web/sites/default/files/".

STEP #5. CHECK THE END RESULT

- **navigate** to the site in your web browser at
  `http://ddevdemo.ddev.site`
- **confirm** that your site is up-and-running with images

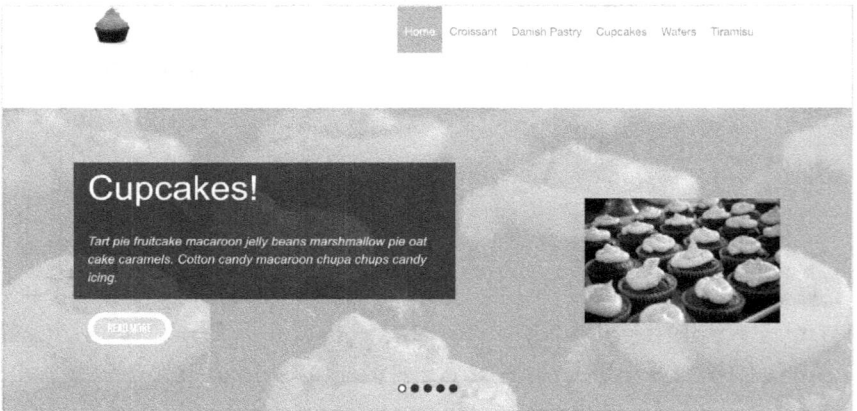

You may need to rebuild caches for the site to properly display. You can do this by logging into the site and then using the `Flush all caches` command from the admin menu.

Here are the admin credentials for the site:

>   Username: admin | Password: admin

WHAT'S NEXT?

In the next chapter, I'll show you how to clone an existing WordPress 5 site to your local machine and get it up-and-running with DDEV-Local.

DDEV-LOCAL COMMAND OVERVIEW

Below is a list of DDEV-Local commands we have covered:

1. `help`
2. `version`
3. `composer`
4. `config`
5. `describe`
6. `launch`
7. `restart`
8. `start`
9. `import-db`
10. `import-files`

CHAPTER 8.

CLONING AN EXISTING WORDPRESS SITE TO DDEV-LOCAL EXPLAINED

In *Installing a New WordPress Site in DDEV-Loval Explained*, I showed you how to get a new WordPress site up-and-running in DDEV-Local using two different methods. In this chapter, we'll be getting an existing WordPress 5 site up-and-running locally. The site is a fairly generic WordPress site with a few posts and uploaded images that I've made available on GitHub.

As the project already exists, you'll want to clone the site from the project's remote repository. This allows you to get an up-to-date copy of the codebase, plus a complete history of the code changes. You will also need to get the site's database and content files (*"uploads", in WordPress parlance*) in order to get the full site up-and-running.

As we have previously learned that DDEV-Local works with Drupal , TYPO3, WordPress, and other applications, in this chapter, we're going to clone a WordPress 5 site.

I've made a codebase, database, and content files directory available for you to practice with:

> https://github.com/ultimike/ddevwordpress.

The codebase is not yet configured to work with DDEV-Local,

so we'll be utilizing the `ddev config` command to get our local environment configured.

The database export is located in the "/db_backup/" directory of the repository.

The "uploads/" directory export is located in the "/uploads_backup/" directory of the repository.

While committing uploads and databases to the project repository is not best practice for an actual project, this is only a demonstration project.

STEP #1. CLONE THE PROJECT

From your local command line, navigate to the directory where you want to clone the project to. Typically, this is your local "sites/" directory. Then, enter this command:

```
$ git clone https://github.com/ultimike/ddevwordpress.git
```

This will clone the entire project's history from GitHub to your computer, in a new directory named *ddevwordpress*. Once cloned, Git will create a working directory of the branch named *master*. The general structure of the git clone command is:

```
git clone protocol://url_of_repository name_of_local_directory_to_create
```

When you omit the `name_of_local_directory_to_create` parameter, the name of the directory is set to the name of the repository, in this case `ddevwordpress`.

After the git clone command is finished, your local "ddevwordpress" directory structure will contain the usual WordPress files as well as /db_backup/ and /uploads_backup/

directories. This site was originally created by downloading the WordPress codebase directly from WordPress.org (*similar to example 1 from the "Installing a New WordPress Site in DDEV-Local Explained" chapter*).

Once the site is successfully cloned,

- **use** `$ cd ddevwordpress` to navigate into the project directory

STEP #2. LAUNCH THE DDEV-LOCAL CONTAINERS

The second step is to use DDEV-Local to get the site up-and-running on your local machine. Keep in mind that DDEV-Local provides a set of Docker containers per project, so the containers will be configured specifically for this project.

- **run** `$ ddev config` from the command line

When you run this command without passing any parameters or flags, it will ask several questions so that DDEV-Local can provide a set of default Docker containers for the project. DDEV-Local will guess the correct answers based on the contents of the project directory; default values will be displayed in parentheses at the end of each question.

- **respond** to DDEV-Local's questions with the following replies:

    1. **Project name:** `ddevwordpress` (*Typically, the project name is set as the same as the project directory name.*)

    2. **Docroot location:** `blank` (*current directory*) (*As this codebase does NOT include a nested docroot, the project root is the same as the document root. DDEV-Local will guess the proper value*

and provide it as an option in the prompt.)

3. **Project type:** wordpress (*DDEV-Local will do its best to figure this out based on the codebase.*)

The entire output of the `ddev config` command should look similar to the following:

```
$ ddev config

Creating a new ddev project config in the current directory
(/Users/michael/sites/ddevwordpress)
Once completed, your configuration will be written to
/Users/michael/sites/ddevwordpress/.ddev/config.yaml

Project name (ddevwordpress):

The docroot is the directory from which your site is
served. This is a relative path from your project root
(/Users/michael/sites/ddevwordpress)
You may leave this value blank if your site files are in
the project root
Docroot Location (current directory):
Found a wordpress codebase at /Users/michael/sites/
ddevwordpress.
Project Type [backdrop, php, drupal6, drupal7, drupal8,
wordpress, typo3] (wordpress):
Configuration complete. You may now run 'ddev start'.
```

- **run** `$ ddev start` from the command line to download, create and run the containers for this project

You may have to enter your computer's password in order for DDEV-Local to add an entry to your *hosts* **file for this project.** The entire output of this command should look similar to the following:

```
$ ddev start
Starting ddevwordpress...
ddev needs to add an entry to your hostfile.
```

```
It will require administrative privileges via the sudo
command, so you may be required
to enter your password for sudo. ddev is about to issue the
command:

sudo /usr/local/bin/ddev hostname ddevwordpress.ddev.site
127.0.0.1

Please enter your password if prompted.

Running Command Command=sudo /usr/local/bin/ddev hostname
ddevwordpress.ddev.site 127.0.0.1
Creating ddev-ddevwordpress-db ... done
Creating ddev-ddevwordpress-dba ... done
Creating ddev-ddevwordpress-web ... done
Network ddev_default is external, skipping
Creating ddev-router ... done
Ensuring write permissions for ddevwordpress
Successfully started ddevwordpress
Project can be reached at http://ddevwordpress.ddev.site,
https://ddevwordpress.ddev.site, http://127.0.0.1:32779
```

At this point, only the project's codebase is ready for you to use. Neither the database nor the "uploads/" directory is ready yet. Visiting one of the URLs provided by DDEV-Local will redirect you to the WordPress installation page. But, since this project includes a database, the next step is to import, not to install, the site's database.

STEP #3. IMPORT THE DATABASE

Now that we have the complete codebase on our local environment with DDEV-Local up-and-running, the next step is to import the database.

- **import** the database provided with this project (*in the "/ddevwordpress/db_backup/" directory*) with the following command

```
$ ddev import-db --src=db_backup/db.sql.gz
```

> A common pitfall with this command occurs when the database dump file has an incorrect extension.
>
> For example, if a database dump file is provided that is compressed, but has the ".sql" extension, this command will fail. The Linux `file` command is helpful in determining the actual file type, regardless of the extension.
>
> ```
> $ file test.sql.gz
>   test.sql.gz: gzip compressed data, max compression, from Unix
> ```

At this point, if you visit one of the local site's URLs, your local copy of the DDEV WordPress site should now load. However, you won't see any uploaded images yet.

STEP #4. PLACE THE CONTENT FILES

Now that we have the codebase and the database on our local environment with DDEV-Local up-and-running, it's time to import our content files. The DDEV WordPress project repository includes an archive of the necessary content files.

- **import** the files into the site using the following `ddev import-files` command

```
$ ddev import-files --src=uploads_backup/uploads.zip
```

This command will simply extract the archive and move it to

the proper location in the codebase, which is "/ddevwordpress/wp-content/uploads/".

STEP #5. CHECK THE END RESULT

- **navigate** to the site in your web browser at `http://ddevwordpress.ddev.site`
- **confirm** that your site is up-and-running with images

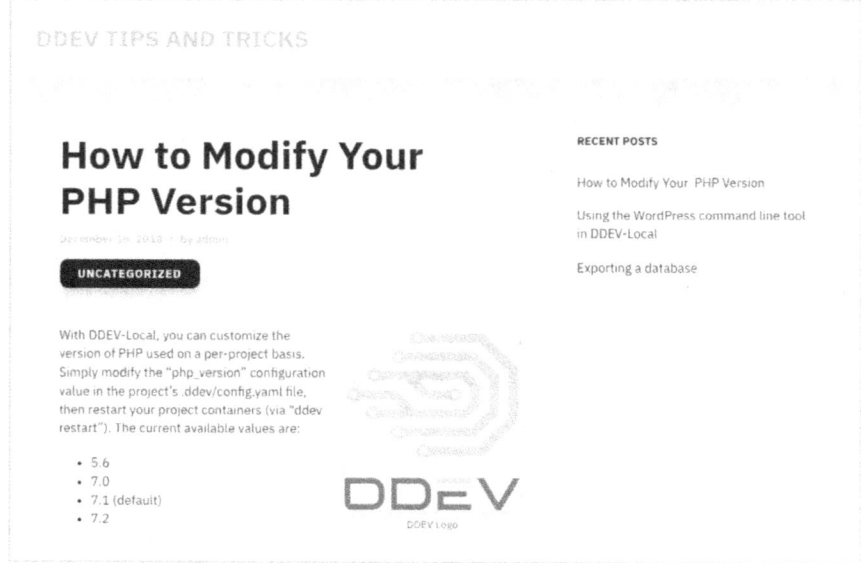

You may need to clear your browser's cache for the site to properly display.

Here are the admin credentials for the site:

> Username: admin | Password: admin

WHAT'S NEXT?

In the next chapter, we'll learn how DDEV-Local can work with remote development environments (*called "providers"*) to provide an easy way to copy a remote database and/or files directory into the local environment.

DDEV-LOCAL COMMAND OVERVIEW

Below is a list of DDEV-Local commands we have covered:

1. `help`
2. `version`
3. `composer`
4. `config`
5. `describe`
6. `launch`
7. `restart`
8. `start`
9. `import-db`
10. `import-files`

CHAPTER 9.

INTEGRATING DDEV-LOCAL WITH A HOSTING PROVIDER

Up to this point, we've been focusing on using DDEV-Local in a vacuum. We've set up a local development environment whose only connection to the outside world is via a remote Git repository.

However, DDEV-Local has a feature called a *provider*. This is a connection to a remote hosting environment. A provider in DDEV-Local allows you to utilize a single DDEV-Local command to import the database and content files from a remote environment. This enables you to keep your local environment up-to-date with a remote environment.

Providers have an API that allows you to connect to the remote environment. They also provide the logic for querying for and downloading database and content files' backups.

You specify a provider in your project's ".ddev/config.yml" file. When you've done that, you can use the `ddev pull` command to pull down the latest backup of a project's database and content files and import it into the local environment.

Currently, the only supported providers for DDEV-Local are DDEV-Live (*currently only for enterprise-level clients*) and

Pantheon (http://pantheon.io). The DDEV team plans to add more providers soon.

In this chapter, I'll show you how to connect DDEV-Local to a site hosted with Pantheon.

> NOTE: This example only works if you're working with a DDEV-Local project that has a remote repository with Pantheon.

STEP #1. AUTHENTICATE WITH THE PROVIDER

This first step only needs to be performed once for your DDEV-Local install. You do not have to do this for every site on your DDEV-Local install.

To use Pantheon as a DDEV-Local provider, your local environment must authenticate via a Pantheon Machine Token.

To generate machine tokens:

- **log in** to Pantheon
- **go to** "Account" tab
- **click** "Machine Tokens" to create new token
- **name** the token something memorable

Keep in mind that Pantheon machine tokens are generally per-application and per-machine. For example, *DDEV-Local on personal laptop* is an example of a name for the new token.

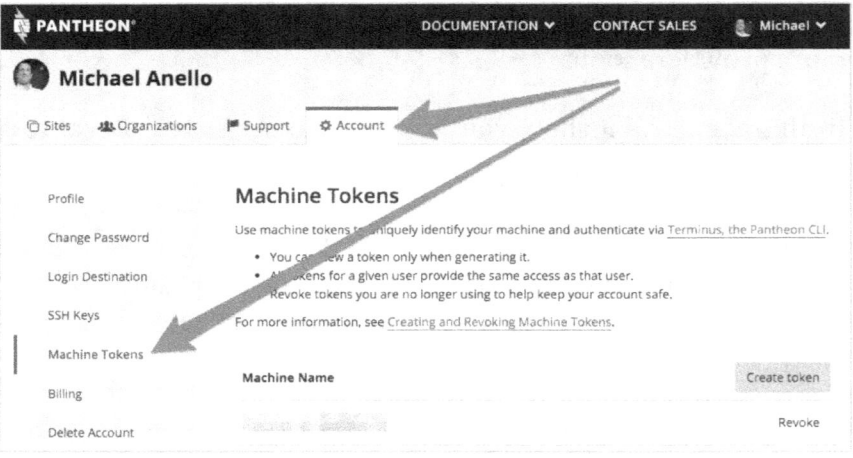

NOTE: This token will only be displayed once. After you navigate off this page, you will NOT be able to view the machine token again, so take care to **save** the machine token in a safe place.

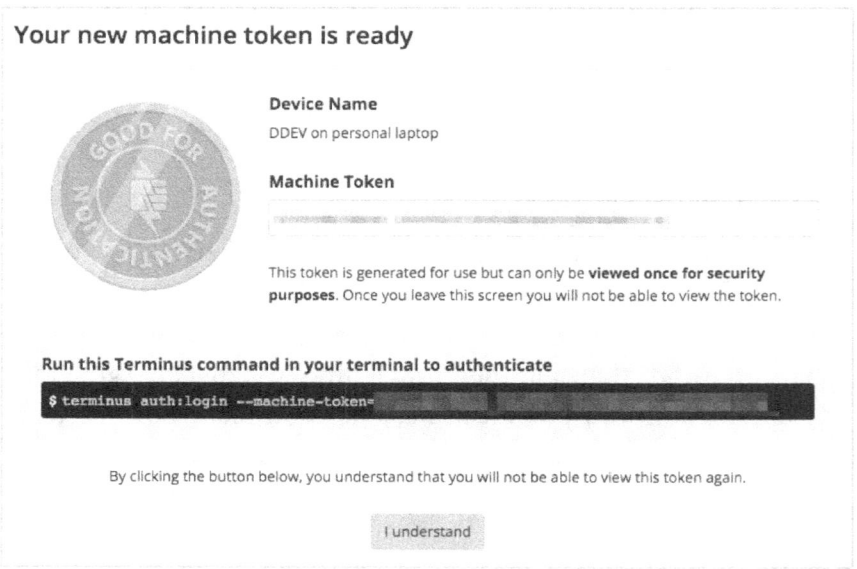

- **copy** the machine token to your clipboard

- **run** the following DDEV-Local command to authenticate DDEV-Local with your Pantheon account
- **replace** {your-pantheon-machine-token} in the code below with the machine token provided to you by Pantheon

```
dev auth pantheon {your-pantheon-machine-token}
```

STEP #2. CONFIGURE YOUR DDEV-LOCAL INSTALL

Use the command line to access the project directory of your existing DDEV-Local site. Now you can re-run the `ddev config` command to update the DDEV-Local configuration for the project. This time, you will pass in the name of the provider.

```
ddev config pantheon
```

This command will configure your local environment to use Pantheon as the provider.

It is required for the site's DDEV-Local project name to be exactly the same as its project machine name on Pantheon. For example, if your Pantheon site's development environment URL is:

```
http://dev-mysuperduperproject.pantheon.site
```

Then your project's Pantheon machine name is "mysuperduperproject"; therefore your DDEV-Local project-name should be "mysuperduperproject", which in turn means that the project directory should also be named "mysuperduperproject".

When you run the `ddev config pantheon` command, notice that it takes a few extra seconds to configure. This is because

DDEV-Local is contacting Pantheon to authenticate and find the corresponding project associated with your account. In addition to the standard `ddev config pantheon` prompts, you will also be asked to configure the *import environment*. This is the Pantheon environment you'd like to pull the database and "files/" directory from when running the `ddev pull` command.

```
Michaels-MacBook-Pro:ddevdemo michael$ ddev config pantheon
You are reconfiguring the project at /Users/michael/sites/ddevdemo.
The existing configuration will be updated and replaced.
Project name (ddevdemo):

The docroot is the directory from which your site is served. This is a relative path
from your project root (/Users/michael/sites/ddevdemo)
You may leave this value blank if your site files are in the project root
Docroot Location (web):
Found a drupal8 codebase at /Users/michael/sites/ddevdemo/web.
Project Type [backdrop, php, drupal6, drupal7, drupal8, wordpress, typo3] (drupal8):

Configure import environment:

        - live
        - dev
        - test

Type the name to select an environment to import from (dev):
Ensuring write permissions for ddevdemo
Existing settings.php file includes settings.ddev.php
Configuration complete. You may now run 'ddev start' or 'ddev pull'
Michaels-MacBook-Pro:ddevdemo michael$
```

STEP #3. USE THE "DDEV PULL" COMMAND

With the first two steps, you've completed the authentication and configuration. You can now utilize the `ddev pull` command to automatically update the local project environment with a copy of the database and content files from your Pantheon environment.

Currently, the `ddev pull` command cannot create a new database and content files backup automatically. So, prior to using the `ddev pull` command, you must first:

- **navigate** to the Pantheon Dashboard for the remote environment
- **click** "Create a New Backup" button

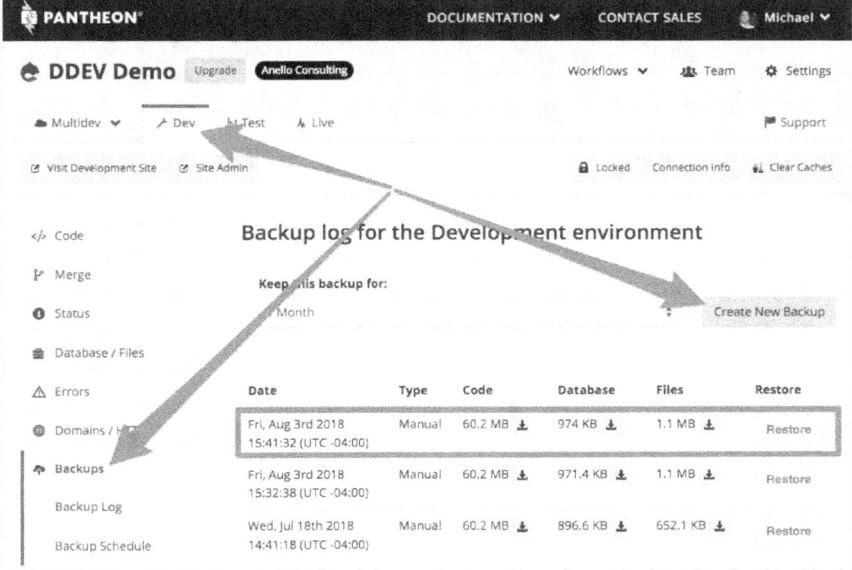

For example, in the previous image, when `ddev pull` is run, it will import the *Database* and *Files* backup from *Fri, Aug 3rd 2018 15:41:32 (UTC -04:00)*. If you desire a more recent backup,

- **click** the "Create New Backup" button to create a current backup

If no backups exist, the `ddev pull` command will fail.

Prior to running the `ddev pull` command, it is important to note that your current local database and content files WILL BE replaced with the database and content files from the remote environment.

> NOTE: If you have non-code work on your local that you would like to keep (*for example, any site configuration or content stored in the database*), do NOT run the `ddev pull` command.

INTEGRATING DDEV-LOCAL WITH A HOSTING PROVIDER 79

- **run** `ddev pull` to download and replace your local database and content files directory with the backup you indicated during the provider configuration

The output of this command should appear be similar to the following:

```
Michaels-MacBook-Pro:ddevdemo michael$ ddev pull
You're about to delete the current database and files and
replace with a fresh import. Would you like to continue (y/
N): y
ddevdemo_dev_2018-08-03T19-41-03_UTC_database.sql.gz
Importing database...
Ensuring write permissions for ddevdemo
Existing settings.php file includes settings.ddev.php
ddevdemo_dev_2018-08-03T19-41-03_UTC_files.tar.gz
Importing files...
Successfully Imported.
Your project can be reached at http://ddevdemo.ddev.site,
https://ddevdemo.ddev.site, http://127.0.0.1:32866
```

- **navigate** to your local site in your browser
- **confirm** that its database and content files are now up-to-date with the remote environment

The `ddev pull` command also has a couple of handy flags that allow you to have the command skip the files directory and/or the database when using the command. For example, to pull down only the latest database backup, use:

```
ddev pull --skip-files
```

TERMINUS COMMAND LINE TOOL

DDEV-Local includes Pantheon's Terminus command line tool (`https://pantheon.io/docs/terminus`) as part of the default *web* container.

It can be accessed just like any other command line tool installed in the *web* container:

```
ddev . terminus env:clear-cache ddevdemo.dev
```

All sites accessible to your Pantheon account are available via Terminus, assuming you authenticated using the `ddev auth pantheon` command mentioned earlier in this chapter.

WHAT'S NEXT?

The ability to easily update local development environments is a valuable tool for web developers. Most modern web developers are proficient enough with Git to keep their local project codebase up-to-date, but sometimes the process for keeping the database and content files up-to-date can be tedious. By utilizing the `ddev pull` command, developers can (*and should!*) get in the habit of not only performing a `git pull` when starting on a new task, but also a `ddev pull` to get the *entire* local development environment up-to-date.

In the next chapter, we'll talk about day-to-day usage of DDEV-Local, including commonly-used commands.

DDEV-LOCAL COMMAND OVERVIEW

Below is a list of DDEV-Local commands we have covered:

1. `help`
2. `version`
3. `composer`
4. `config`
5. `describe`

6. launch
7. restart
8. start
9. import-db
10. import-files
11. auth
12. pull

CHAPTER 10.

USING THE MOST COMMON DDEV-LOCAL COMMANDS

In the last few chapters, I've introduced you to many of the DDEV-Local commands. In this chapter, I'll show you how to use these (*and some additional*) commands to take full control of your DDEV-Local-based projects.

This chapter will provide an overview of a typical daily workflow of working on a DDEV-Local-powered project.

STARTING AND STOPPING YOUR DDEV-LOCAL PROJECT

When you're ready to work on a DDEV-Local-based project, the first thing to do is to ensure that Docker is up-and-running. Depending on your operating system, this may involve launching Docker for Windows/Mac, or running the Docker daemon.

You should only run DDEV-Local project containers when you're working on a project. Containers consume valuable system resources, and so I recommend stopping them when you're not working.

When you're ready to start,

- **navigate** using the command line to the directory for the project you'd like to work on

- **run** ddev start

This command will spin up your project's containers. This command is similar to launching a program on your desktop. Once this task completes, DDEV-Local will present you with the local URLs with which you can access your site.

At this point, you can work on your project as if you're using any other local development environment. You can add files, edit files, modify the database, or do whatever else your current task calls for.

- **run** ddev ssh to connect to the *web* container if you need to run a command line tool for your project

By default, this command will connect to the *web* container. However, by using a "-service <service>" flag, you can connect to any of the DDEV-Local containers for your project (*db, and dba, by default*). Once connected, you can run one of the command line tools provided by the default DDEV-Local *web* container (*Composer, Drush, Drupal Console, npm, wp-cli, Git, apt, among others*), or anything that is part of your codebase.

After this command is run, the command line prompt will likely be different, as in the following image.

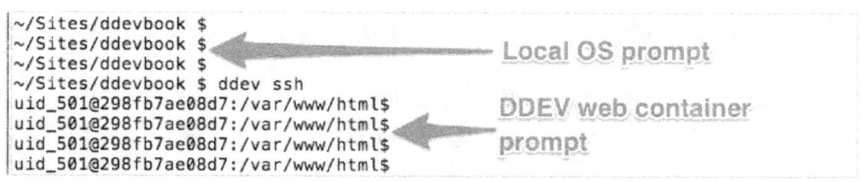

> REMEMBER: DDEV-Local utilizes Docker

> containers, which are each self-contained Linux machines. So, when you use the `ddev ssh` command, it is similar to connecting to a remote server that has its own file system.
>
> So, the full path to the codebase inside the container will be different than the full path on your host operating system. Docker keeps track of all this and keeps the codebase synced between the two.

- **use** `exit` to exit the *web* container and return to your local command line
- **run** `ddev stop` to stop and remove the project's containers when you're done working on a project (*and the end of your work day*)

This is similar to quitting a desktop application.

Removing your project's containers will NORMALLY NOT lead to any data loss. Remember, your project directory is synced between your host OS and the DDEV-Local web container. Removing the containers (*including the web container*) does NOT remove your project directory on your host OS.

Similarly, your project database exists in a Docker volume. Removing your project's db container will NOT remove the Docker volume where your database is kept. When you start your project back up again, the weband db containers will simply re-connect to your project directory and Docker (*database*) volume.>

One situation where you could have data loss is if you have added packages, code, or any files to any of the project's containers outside of the project directory. In this case, they will NOT be synced back to your host OS, and they WILL BE lost when the container is removed.

In these situations, it is best to utilize a DDEV-Local command hook to automatically add what you need whenever the container is started.

- **run** `ddev delete` from the project's directory if you'd like to completely remove a DDEV-Local project from your local environment (*including its database volume*)

This is the same as: `ddev stop --remove-data`

This will remove the project's containers, its hostnames, as well as the project's Docker database volumes.

At this point, it is safe to also delete the project directory from your file system to completely remove the project from your computer. When you run this command, a database snapshot will be created and stored in the ".ddev/db_snapshots/" directory of your project.

> Add the "–omit-snapshot" option to either the `ddev delete` or `ddev stop` command to prevent the database snapshot from being created.

- **run** `ddev pause` to simply pause the project's containers instead of removing them
- **use** `ddev list` to confirm that you don't have any DDEV-Local projects running (*more on this command below*)

This command will show you a list of projects that are running, stopped, or paused.

> It is recommended that prior to quitting Docker, or restarting your computer, you confirm that no projects are running.

- **use** ddev poweroff to stop ALL running DDEV-local projects (*as well as the "ssh-agent maintenance" container*)

Regardless of which method you utilize to end your work session with your project (ddev stop, ddev remove, *or* ddev pause), when you're ready to work on the project again, use the ddev start command to get the containers up-and-running again.

RUNNING COMPOSER COMMANDS WITH DDEV-LOCAL

In a previous chapter, we saw how we can use the ddev composer create command to run Composer's create-project command inside a DDEV-Local *web* container. Virtually any other Composer command can be run via the ddev composer command as well. For example:

```
ddev composer update vendor/project --with-dependencies
ddev composer remove vendor/project
ddev composer require vendor/project --prefer-dist
ddev composer install<
```

ACCESSING THE DATABASE VIA THE COMMAND LINE

Do you need to run SQL commands via the command line? While you could access the DDEV database container with:

```
ddev ssh -s=db
```

You could also directly access the SQL command line using:

```
ddev mysql
```

This connects you directly to your project's default database (*use* `exit` *to return to your host operating system*). This command is implemented as a DDEV custom command (*see the ".ddev/ commands/ directory of your project"*).

USING OTHER SOFTWARE WITH DDEV-LOCAL

Do you need to access a database client for your project? DDEV-Local includes a *dba* container with phpMyAdmin (`https://phpmyadmin.net`) configured to access the project's database.

- **run** `ddev describe` to have the URL displayed

In the *Other Services* section of the output, you should see something like the following:

```
Other Services
--------------
MailHog: http://myproject.ddev.site:8025
phpMyAdmin: http://myproject.ddev.site:8036
```

- **navigate** to the phpMyAdmin URL to access your database (*or use* `ddev launch -p`).

The default database name for any DDEV-Local project is *db*, so when you are navigating inside of phpMyAdmin, look for the database shown in the image below.

If you're using Mac OS X and utilize the native MySql/MariaDB database client Sequel Pro (https://sequelpro.com),

- **run** `ddev sequelpro` to launch Sequel Pro and automatically connect to your project's database

DDEV-Local also provides the email testing tool, MailHog (https://github.com/mailhog/MailHog). You can use this tool to review and test outgoing emails from your project. Mailhog acts as an email interceptor to capture outgoing emails from your local development environment and display them in a webmail interface.

As before, you can utilize the output from `ddev describe` to determine the URL for your project's MailHog interface.

```
Other Services
--------------
MailHog: http://myproject.ddev.site:8025
phpMyAdmin: http://myproject.ddev.site:8036
```

- **navigate** to the MailHog URL to access your outgoing email (*or use* `ddev launch -m`)

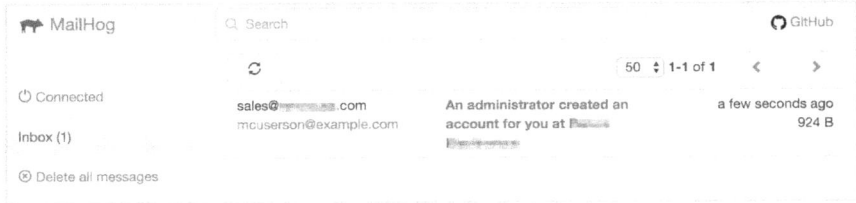

Once captured by MailHog, you have the option to release any message to its intended recipient.

LISTING DDEV-LOCAL PROJECTS

It can be easy to forget which of your DDEV-Local projects are running, paused, or stopped. If you accidentally quit Docker while a DDEV-Local project is running, it can corrupt your local database, forcing you to reimport.

- **use** `ddev list` to see a list of all your DDEV-Local projects and their current status (*running, paused,* or *stopped*) to help avoid corrupting your local database

If you have projects that you don't want displayed in the list (*projects you don't use very often, for example*), remove them from the list by using: `ddev stop --unlist`

LEVERAGING DATABASE SNAPSHOTS

DDEV-Local introduced the concept of a database snapshot in version 1.1 of DDEV-Local. Database snapshots are not SQL dump files, rather they are copies of the file structure of the Docker volume that contains the database structure and data. During a project's development, it can be very useful to take a *snapshot* of the database at different points in time, in case it would be useful to roll-back the database to a previous snapshot.

By default, when the `ddev snapshot` command is run with no flags, the snapshot's name includes a timestamp. It is advised to utilize the `--name` flag to give snapshots a more descriptive name. For example:

```
ddev snapshot --name=before_drupal_86_update
```

DDEV-Local stores snapshots in the project's `.ddev/db_snapshots/` directory.

> You may consider adding the ".ddev/db_snapshots/" directory to your project's ".gitignore" file so database snapshots are NOT part of your project's history.

The `restore-snapshot` command works as advertised, just provide it with a name of a snapshot to restore to.

```
ddev restore-snapshot before_drupal_86_update
```

> NOTE: The `ddev restore-snapshot` command triggers a `ddev restart` (*including a* `ddev stop`), while the `ddev snapshot` command does NOT.

As an extra safety feature, the `ddev stop --remove-data` command triggers a `ddev snapshot` automatically.

WHAT'S NEXT?

In this chapter, we talked about basic DDEV-Local workflows as well as some other helpful DDEV-Local commands. In the next chapter, we'll learn how to extend some of the basic DDEV-Local commands so that we can customize their behavior.

DDEV-LOCAL COMMAND OVERVIEW

Below is a list of DDEV-Local commands we have covered:

1. `help`
2. `version`
3. `composer`
4. `config`
5. `describe`
6. `launch`
7. `restart`
8. `start`
9. `import-db`
10. `import-files`
11. `auth`
12. `pull`
13. `delete`
14. `list`
15. `mysqul`
16. `poweroff`
17. `pause`
18. `restore-snapshot`
19. `sequelpro`

20. snapshot
21. ssh
22. stop

CHAPTER 11.

EXTENDING AND CREATING CUSTOM DDEV-LOCAL COMMANDS EXPLAINED

In this chapter, we're going to dive deeper into DDEV-Local commands.

You can extend several DDEV-Local commands by adding additional tasks, which you can perform either before or after the DDEV-Local command is run. For example, you can run custom tasks before or after you execute the `ddev start` command. You add these custom tasks via the project's ".ddev/config.yaml" file. As with all changes to the ".ddev/config.yaml" file, you will need to run `ddev restart` for any command hook changes to take effect.

You can also create brand new custom commands for any of your DDEV containers that can be run using the simple `ddev my-command` syntax (*where* `my-command` *is your custom command*).

EXTENDING DDEV-LOCAL COMMANDS
There are multiple DDEV-local commands that you can extend:

1. `ddev start`
2. `ddev import-db`

3. `ddev import-files`
4. `ddev composer`
5. `ddev config`
6. `ddev stop`
7. `ddev exec`
8. `ddev pause`
9. `ddev pull`
10. `ddev snapshot`
11. `ddev restore-snapshot`

You can extend each of these commands with both pre- and post- tasks. This means that 22 *command hooks* are available. For example, command hooks for the `start`, `import-db`, and `pull` commands are:

1. `pre-start`
2. `post-start`
3. `pre-import-db`
4. `post-import-db`
5. `pre-pull`
6. `post-pull`

There are two types of tasks than you can add to command hooks:

1. `exec`: commands that are run in the *web* container. For example, use `exec --service=db` to run the command in the *db* container.
2. `exec-host`: commands that are run in the host operating system.

COMMAND HOOK EXAMPLES

Command hooks are placed in a project's ".ddev/config.yaml" file, and they use the folllowing format:

```
hooks:
post-start:
- exec: "drush cr"
```

Let's take a look at some sample command hooks. First, if you're working with a Drupal site, this will provide the admin login on start:

```
hooks:
post-start:
- exec: drush uli
```

Second, this command hook will get your Drupal site ready after a database import on start. Reading this command: after an `import-db` is run, rebuild caches, run any database and entity updates, run cron.

```
hooks:
post-import-db:
- exec: drush cr
- exec: drush updb
- exec: drush entup
- exec: drush cron
```

This third sample command is for a Drupal site on a Mac OS X host. This hook will get your site ready for development on start. This example uses a combination of `exec` and `exec-host` tasks to rebuild caches, run database updates, run entity updates, run cron, open the default browser to the site, and open the site in PhpStorm.

```
hooks:
```

```
post-start:
 - exec: drush cr
 - exec: drush updb
 - exec: drush entup
 - exec: drush cron
 - exec: drush en -y stage_file_proxy
 - exec-host: open http://myproject.ddev.site
 - exec-host: phpstorm .
```

This fourth sample command will install a Composer-based project, on `start`:

```
hooks:
post-start:
 - exec: composer install
```

CREATING A CUSTOM COMMAND

Custom DDEV commands behave just like the commands that DDEV comes with. By creating a custom command, you can call it using standard DDEV syntax!

> Custom commands are basically bash scripts that can be associated with any of your project's containers as well as your host operating system.

Custom commands live in your project's ".ddev/commands/" directory – each command lives in the subdirectory corresponding to the container where it will run. For example, the `ddev mysql` command is just a custom command – you can see it in your project's ".ddev/commands/db/" directory.

In this example, we'll create a new custom `drupal-local`

command that generates and conditionally includes a Drupal "settings.local.php" file.

- **create** a new "drupal-local" (*no extension*) file in ".ddev/commands/web/" directory. This command will run in the *web* container.
- **add** the following code to the "drupal-local" file:

```
#!/bin/bash## Description: Create a Drupal
settings.local.php file.
## Usage: drupal-local
## Example: "ddev drupal-local" if grep -q
'settings.local.php' '/var/www/html/web/sites/default/
settings.php';then
    echo "It appears the settings.local.php file is already
ready for use."
else
    cp /var/www/html/web/sites/example.settings.local.php
/var/www/html/web/sites/default/settings.local.php
    #sed -i '/#ddev-generated/i if (file_exists(\$app_root .
\'/\' . \$site_path . \'\/settings.local.php\')) {\n
include \$app_root . \'/\' . \$site_path .
\'\/settings.local.php\';\n}\n' /var/www/html/web/sites/
default/settings.php
    #cd /var/www/html/web/sites/default
    sed -i "/ddev-generated/i if (file_exists(\$app_root .
'/' . \$site_path . \'\/settings.local.php\')) {\n  include
\$app_root . \'/\' . \$site_path .
\'\/settings.local.php\';\n}\n" /var/www/html/web/sites/
default/settings.php
    echo "The settings.local.php has been configured."
fi
exit 0
```

Note that the "Usage" line of the code defines the command name, not the file name (*although it is a good idea to keep them the same*). The text in the "Example" line will be output when users use the `--help` option when running the command.

This custom command uses the *grep* tool to check if the string "settings.local.php" exists in the project's "settings.php" file. If so, it exits. If not, it uses the `cp` command to copy the "example.settings.local.php" file (*provided by Drupal core*) to the proper directory then uses `sed` to add a conditional include to the "settings.php" file **before** the conditional include for the "settings.ddev.php" file.

- **run** your new custom command with `ddev drupal-local`

WHAT'S NEXT?

In this chapter, we learned how we can customize several of the basic DDEV-Local commands by running additional tasks either before or after you run the command. In the next chapter, I'll cover some tips and tricks that I've learned while using DDEV-Local on a day-to-day basis. Some of the topics we'll be covering include updating DDEV-Local, utilizing alternate host names, and trouble-shooting port conflicts.

DDEV-LOCAL COMMAND OVERVIEW

Below is a list of DDEV-Local commands we have covered:

1. `help`
2. `version`
3. `composer`
4. `config`
5. `describe`
6. `launch`
7. `restart`
8. `start`
9. `import-db`

10. import-files
11. auth
12. pull
13. delete
14. list
15. mysqul
16. poweroff
17. pause
18. restore-snapshot
19. sequelpro
20. snapshot
21. ssh
22. stop

CHAPTER 12.

USEFUL DDEV-LOCAL TIPS AND TRICKS EXPLAINED

In previous chapters, we've seen how to install, configure, and use DDEV-Local on a day-to-day basis.

This chapter will provide you with tips and tricks that you can use to complete other key tasks with DDEV-Local. Specifically, you will learn how to:

1. export a database
2. use the DDEV-Local `exec` command
3. solve port conflicts with DDEV-Local
4. use additional project hostnames
5. modify your PHP version
6. override PHP and other server configuration values
7. update DDEV-Local
8. utilize NFS mounting for better performance on Mac OS X and Windows 10
9. utilize https for DDEV-local project by default (*with no hassle!*)
10. add files to a project's *web* container's home directory

HOW TO EXPORT A DATABASE

In an earlier chapter, we saw how you can use the `ddev import-db` command to IMPORT a database INTO the DDEV-Local db container. There is a corresponding command to EXPORT a database FROM the DDEV-Local *db* container:

  ddev export-db –file=/path/to/file.sql.gz

> NOTE: This command exports the database as a compressed file, so be sure to save the export using a ".sql.gz" extension.

In addition, you can also utilize the `mysqldump` command via the DDEV-Local *web* container. You can do this using the command below.

  ddev exec mysqldump db > db.sql

In this example, the default *db* database is exported to the *web* directory in the project root named "db.sql".

Finally, you can also use the "Export" feature tab inside phpMyAdmin. As a reminder, you can access the *dba* container via the URL provided by the `ddev describe` command. We showed you how to access phpMyAdmin in the chapter, *How to Use the Most Common DDEV-Local Commands*.

HOW TO USE THE DDEV-LOCAL "EXEC" COMMAND

You can use the `ddev exec` command to run a command directly in one of the project's Docker containers without using the `ddev ssh` command first.

By default, the `ddev exec` command runs the provided command in the *web* container. To run a command in one of the other project containers, you can use the `--service` (*or* `-s`) flag.

For example, to run a command in the *db* container, use: `ddev exec -s db <command>`

> Save yourself a few keystrokes by using a period instead of the word `exec`. For example: `ddev . drush cron` or `ddev . wp cron test` are equivalent to `ddev exec drush cron` and `ddev exec wp cron test`

Starting with DDEV-Local 1.16.0, the following command line tools are included with DDEV-Local and can be run directly without using `exec` or `.` :

1. `typo3`
2. `typo3cms`
3. `drush`
4. `artisan`
5. `magento`
6. `wp`

HOW TO SOLVE PORT CONFLICTS WITH DDEV-LOCAL

Sometimes, when starting a DDEV-Local project with `ddev`

`start`, an error will occur and the following message will be displayed:

```
Failed to start <project name>: Unable to listen on
required ports, localhost port 80 is in use.
```

This is an indication that there is some other process on your machine that is utilizing port 80. Usually, this means that there is another web server up-and-running on your machine; simply quitting it should do the trick.

Sometimes, it isn't clear what the other process is that is using the conflicted port. In these cases, edit the project's ".ddev/config.yaml" file and modify the "router_http_port" and "router_https_port" values, then try the `ddev start` command again.

For example, in the ".ddev/config.yaml" file, change:

```
router_http_port: "80"
router_https_port: "443"
```

to:

```
router_http_port: "8080"
router_https_port: "8443"
```

HOW TO USE ADDITIONAL PROJECT HOSTNAMES

DDEV-Local provides the ability to provide additional local hostnames for your projects. These are hostnames in addition to the default hostnames provided by default:

```
http://<project-name>.ddev.site
```

```
https://<prcject-name>.ddev.site
```

By manually configuring additional hostnames in the ".ddev/config.yaml" file, you can use additional hostnames to access the local site through a browser. This can be useful for multisite projects, projects that utilize subdomains, and projects where functionality (*usually security-related*) depends on a specific domain name.

There are two types of additional project host names that you can add:

1. Standard host names end in `.ddev.site`
2. Fully qualified domain names (fqdn) can have any top-level domain name that you wish.

Use FQDN with caution, because these can prevent you from reaching the *real* domain. For example, if you set a FQDN for a DDEV-Local project to be espn.com, only your local project will be available at that domain name, not the actual espn.com.

To add additional hostnames to your project, modify your ".ddev/config.yaml" file as follows:

```
APIVersion: v1.0.0
name: ddevdemo
type: drupal8
docroot: web
php_version: "7.1"
router_http_port: "80"
router_https_port: "443"
xdebug_enabled: false
additional_hostnames:
- en.ddevdemo
- nl.ddevdemo
- it.ddevdemo
additional_fqdns:
```

```
- ddevdemo.com
- ddevdemo.net
```

For example, after editing the ".ddev/config.yaml" file as shown above, and doing a `ddev restart`, you can access the local site at the following domain names on your local machine:

1. `en.ddevdemo.ddev.site`
2. `nl.ddevdemo.ddev.site`
3. `it.ddevdemo.ddev.site`
4. `ddevdemo.com`
5. `ddevdemo.net`

It should be noted that there is a `ddev hostname` command that you can use to add additional hostnames directly to the local machine's hosts file. In early versions of DDEV-Local, this was necessary on Windows 10, but recent releases of DDEV-Local have removed the need for this step, so this command isn't necessary.

You can use the `--remove-inactive` flag to purge any DDEV-Local-related hostnames from your local hosts file (*the use of* `sudo` *is normally required for this command*):

```
sudo ddev hostname --remove-inactive
```

HOW TO MODIFY YOUR PHP VERSION

With DDEV-Local, you can customize the version of PHP used on a per-project basis.

- **modify** the "php_version" configuration value in the project's ".ddev/config.yaml" file

- **use** `ddev restart` to restart your project containers

The current available values are:

- 5.6
- 7.0
- 7.1
- 7.2 (*default*)
- 7.3
- 7.4
- 8.0

HOW TO OVERRIDE PHP AND OTHER SERVER CONFIGURATION VALUES

DDEV-Local allows you to customize your local development environments by overriding variables normally found in the "php.ini" file. While it is possible to directly edit the "php.ini" file in the DDEV-Local *web* container, the changes would only affect the current container and would be lost if that container were to be rebuilt (`ddev stop` then `ddev start`).

Instead, developers can create a new ".ddev/php/my-php.ini" file for overrides. For example, to override PHP's memory limit, the "my-php.ini" file would look like the following:

```
[php]
memory_limit = 256M
```

You can override the configuration values for both the default NGINX web server and MariaDB database server in a similar manner by creating the following files in the ".ddev/" directory for the project.

```
.ddev/nginx-site.conf

.ddev/mysql/*.cnf
```

Be sure to perform a `ddev restart` after making any changes to configuration values.

For additional details, see: `https://ddev.readthedocs.io/en/latest/users/extend/customization-extendibility/`.

HOW TO USE APACHE INSTEAD OF NGINX AS THE WEB SERVER IN THE "WEB" CONTAINER

By default, the DDEV-Local *web* container is configured to use NGINX for the web server. If your project requires the use of the Apache web server, there's a simple configuration change you can make to your project's ".ddev/config.yaml" file.

- **change** the `webserver_type` key from `nginx-fpm` to either `apache-fpm` or `apache-cgi`

```
APIVersion: v1.4.1
name: myproject
type: drupal8
docroot: web
php_version: "7.1"
webserver_type: apache-fpm
router_http_port: "80"
router_https_port: "443"
xdebug_enabled: false
additional_hostnames: []
additional_fqdns: []
provider: default
```

As with any change made to DDEV-Local's configuration, once you restart your project's containers the changes will be applied.

HOW TO USE YOUR SSH KEYS FROM WITHIN THE "WEB" CONTAINER

Sometimes it is useful to be able to use ssh keys from your host operating system from within the *web* container. This can be especially useful if you are looking to securely access a remote Git repository or utilize a file syncing tool like rsync from within the *web* container.

DDEV-Local provides a `ddev-ssh-agent` container that is automatically spun up when any DDEV-Local project is running (*not unlike how the ddev-router container operates*). This container provides a mechanism to share your host operating system's ssh keys with your DDEV-Local *web* containers.

To take advantage of this feature, simply run the following command to authenticate your host operating system keys in the *ddev-ssh-agent* container:

```
ddev auth ssh
```

You'll be prompted for your private key passphrase (*if you have one*) when running this command. Once complete, you'll be able to access remote servers from inside the *web* container via ssh as if you're connecting from your local host prompt.

HOW TO UTILIZE LOCAL DDEV CONFIGURATION SETTINGS

If you're working in a team environment, something there is a need to have configuration settings for your local DDEV-Local environment that are NOT shared with the rest of the team.

For example, if your local machine requires you to use http port 8080 while the rest of the team uses port 80, then it would be beneficial if you could have your own local DDEV-Local configuration settings file that isn't part of the project's repository.

This is possible using DDEV-Local's custom "config.*.yaml" files functionality. Any "config.*.yaml" file in your ".ddev/" directory will get loaded after the "config.yaml" file and any variables set in a "config.*.yaml" file will override any variable in the "config.yaml" file.

For example, consider the case where a local developer wants to use http port 8080 as well as implement a post-start hook. A ".ddev/config.local.yaml" file can be created and populated with:

```
router_http_port: "8080"
hooks:
post-start:
- exec: drush cr
- exec: drush updb
- exec: drush cron
```

The "local" part of the filename could be anything – in fact, you can even utilize multiple "config.*.yaml" files (*they will be loaded and parsed alphabetically*). No changes to the ".ddev/config.yaml" file are necessary to take advantage of this feature.

> The `.ddev/.gitignore` is set to ignore any "config.*.yaml" files.

Then, in your local environment, when the project containers are started, http port 8080 will be used only in your local environment, and the post-start exec commands will be run (*again, only in your environment*).

GLOBAL DDEV-LOCAL SETTINGS

DDEV-Local provides a global settings file that affects all DDEV-Local projects on the host operating system, located at "~/.ddev/global_config.yaml".

Available settings include:

`omit_containers` -this array specifies any containers that you would not like to have created for all DDEV-Local projects. This is commonly used to suppress the creation of the *dba* container. You can accomplish this with the following command:

```
ddev config global --omit-containers=dba
```

Or, you can edit the the "global_config.yaml" file directly with:

```
omit_containers:
 - dba
```

It is also possible to omit the database container at the project level (*which also omits the dba container*) by adding `omit_containers[db]` to a project's ".ddev/config.yaml" file.

`instrumentation_opt_in` – this boolean controls whether or not diagnostic information is automatically sent back to Drud Technology during normal DDEV-Local usage. Developers can opt-out of sharing data by setting the value of this configuration parameter to *false*.

HOW TO UPDATE DDEV-LOCAL

Keeping your installation of DDEV-Local up-to-date is an important task, but also fairly straightforward. Remember, DDEV-Local utilizes Docker, so it is also important to keep your Docker installation up-to-date as well.

Keep in mind that when you update DDEV-Local, you'll also want to update each of the DDEV-Local projects on your machine. This is because each project's DDEV-Local configuration is associated with the version of DDEV-Local that configured it. Normally, the process of updating a DDEV-Local project is as simple as re-running the ddev config command and then doing a ddev restart.

As with any software, prior to updating DDEV-Local, it is a good idea to review the release notes for the current release. Release notes for DDEV-Local can be found at https://github.com/drud/ddev/releases. Sometimes the DDEV-Local development team will recommend updating to the latest version of Docker in the DDEV-Local release notes.

Mac OS X

If DDEV-Local was installed using (*the recommended*) Homebrew,

- **use** brew upgrade ddev to update DDEV-Local
- **follow** the prompts to complete the update

If you didn't use Homebrew to install DDEV-Local on Mac OS X,

- **follow** the instructions on the official documentation:

    https://ddev.readthedocs.io/en/latest/#installationupgrade-script-linux-and-macos.

Windows 10

If you installed DDEV-Local using Chocolately,

- **use** choco upgrade ddev

If you used the Windows 10 DDEV-Local installer, then the upgrade process is identical to the installation process.

- **download** the latest version of the installer from
  https://github.com/drud/ddev/releases
- **run** it

Linux (Ubuntu)

If DDEV-Local was installed using (*the recommended*) Linuxbrew,

- **use** brew upgrade ddev to update DDEV-Local

If you didn't use Linuxbrew to install DDEV-Local on Ubuntu,

- **follow** the instructions on the official documentation:

  https://ddev.readthedocs.io/en/latest/#manual-installation-or-upgrade-linux-and-macos.

HOW TO RUN DDEV-LOCAL WITHOUT AN INTERNET CONNECTION

As long as your project isn't configured to use a remote provider (*currently only Pantheon or DDEV-Live are supported*), then DDEV-Local project environments should work just fine without an internet connection. If your project does use a remote provider, then temporarily reconfigure your project without a provider and you should be good-to-go. Once you are back online, simply reconfigure your project with the provider.

TIPS ON KEEPING DOCKER RUNNING SMOOTHLY

Randy Fay, one of the DDEV-Local maintainers offers some helpful tips to keep Docker running smoothly. With his permission, I'm sharing them here.

1. `ddev stop; ddev config; ddev start` after updating DDEV-Local to a new version.
2. `docker stop $(docker ps -q) && docker rm -f $(docker ps -aq)` if a container is hanging or not working as suspected.
3. When all else fails, restart Docker.
4. When #3 doesn't fix the issue, do a Docker factory reset (*and make sure it is up-to-date!*)

UTILIZING NFS MOUNTING FOR BETTER PERFORMANCE

One of the chief complaints of using a Docker-based local development environment like DDEV-Local is performance. The fact that containers are small virtual machines, combined with the fact that syncing the file system between the host OS (*Mac OS X, Windows 10*) and the *web* container can be slow leads to the situation where performance is often slower than native local development environment solutions.

The syncing of the codebase between the host OS and the DDEV *web* container is often a choke point. Remember, your host OS and the *web* container aren't sharing your project directory – they are two separate entities. Docker's default mount syncs changes between the two in real time. So, if you make a code change in your IDE on your host OS, Docker will (*silently, in the background*) sync that change with the same file in the *web* container.

Normally, when you're just modifying just one file at a time, Docker's default syncing is fast enough that you won't notice. But, what if there's an operation that changes lots of files in a very short period of time (*building cache files, for example*)? Docker's default mount can get bogged down and slow your project down. This is where NFS comes in.

NFS (*Network File System*) is an alternative (*and much faster*) method for mounting host OS directories to Docker containers. It's not new technology; in fact, it has its beginnings many years ago as a standard way of sharing file systems in Unix.

Once configured, it can lead to drastic improvements in performance of your local development environment. The downside? There's a one-time setup that differs depending on it you're on Mac OS X or Windows.

> NFS isn't really necessary if your host OS is Linux, as the default Linux Docker mount is plenty fast.

Mac OS X provides *nfsd* (*NFS daemon*), so all we need to do it utilize it. Windows does NOT provide an NFS service by default, but the the Windows installer of DDEV-Local includes one.

In both cases, some minor configuration is required as well – but the DDEV folks have provided a script for each OS, so it's actually quite simple. In both cases, the script does two things:

1. Configures a configuration file that specifies which directories are available to be mounted using NFS.
2. Configures and starts NFS.

By default the NFS setup scripts for Mac OS X and Windows use your entire home directory in the NFS configuration. I would suggest modifying it to something more specific. For example, if all your DDEV projects are located in your "~/sites/" directory, then I would suggest to only mount your "~/sites/" directory (*detailed below*).

> Configuring and using NFS does NOT require you to recreate your local DDEV projects nor put any of your data at risk.

Setting up NFS on Mac OS X

Mac OS X includes *nfsd* by default, and the configuration file can be found at /etc/exports. This is a simple text file that lists the directories that can be mounted via NFS. If you have used Vagrant (or another tool that utilizes NFS) in the past, your /etc/exports file might already have some entries. If that the case, you might run into an issue of overlaps – more on that later.

- **give** Terminal (*or whatever your command line tool of choice is*) full disk access (*via the Mac OS Security and Privacy system preference*)

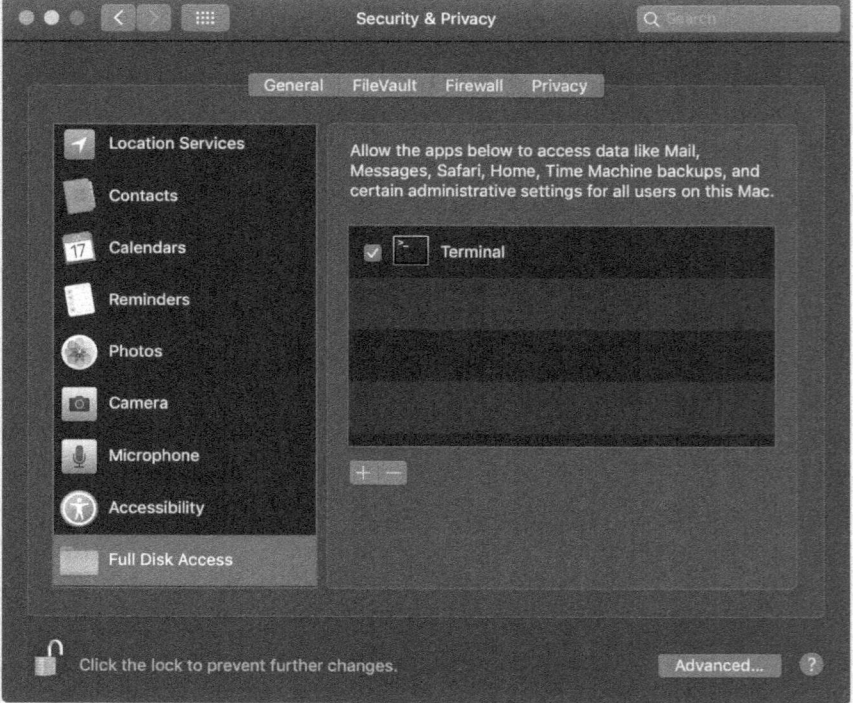

- **download** the Mac OS X DDEV NFS setup script from `https://raw.githubusercontent.com/drud/ddev/master/scripts/macos_ddev_nfs_setup.sh` to your "~/Downloads/" directory

For those of you interested in seeing exactly what the 50-line script does, you'll notice that the first 24 lines are just checks to ensure that 1) you're running it on Mac OS X, 2) you're not running it as the root user, and 3) that Docker is up-and-running. After that, the script stops all of your DDEV-Local projects.

The next section adds your user directory to the "/etc/exports" configuration, then a small configuration change is made to the NFS mount settings.

Finally, the *nsfd* daemon is restarted.

- **run** the script using `sh ~/Downloads/macos_ddev_nfs_setup.sh`

If you want to use a more specific directory in your "/etc/exports" configuration, then edit your "/etc/exports" configuration and change the path. In my case, I changed this code:

```
/Users/michael -alldirs -mapall=501:20 localhost
```

To be this code:

```
/Users/michael/sites -alldirs -mapall=501:20 localhost
```

- **use** `sudo nfsd restart` to restart *nfsd* if you changed your "/etc/exports" file in the previous step
- **update** a DDEV project to use NFS by editing its ".ddev/config.yaml" to include `nfs_mount_enabled: true`

USEFUL DDEV-LOCAL TIPS AND TRICKS EXPLAINED 117

- **use** `ddev start` to start your project
- **confirm** NFS mount is working with `ddev debug nfsmount`

If successful, you should see something like this:

```
$ ddev debug nfsmount Successfully accessed NFS mount of
/Users/michael/sites/mysite
```

- **remove** full disk access from Terminal (*or whatever your command line tool of choice is*) via the Mac OS Security and Privacy system preference.

That's it! As described above, this is a one-time setup, so for any DDEV projects you'd like to use NFS with (*all of them!*) simply add `nfs_mount_enabled: true` to the project's ".ddev/config.yaml" file. The next time you start the project you should be all set!

Setting up NFS on Windows

As mentioned above, Windows 10 does not include an NFS mounting service by default. The Windows DDEV-Local installer includes the components (*winnsfd* and *nssm*) necessary, so all you need to do is run the setup script (below). The script configures *nssm* as a service, utilizing the "~/.ddev/nfs_exports.txt" file for its configuration.

- **download** the Windows DDEV-Local NFS setup script from `https://raw.githubusercontent.com/drud/ddev/master/scripts/windows_ddev_nfs_setup.sh` to your "~/Downloads/" directory.

For those of you interested in seeing exactly what the 64-line script does, you'll notice that the first 44 lines are just checks to ensure that 1) Docker is up-and-running, and 2) the winnsfd and nssm components are available.

After that, the script checks to see if the "~/.ddev/nfs_exports.txt" configuration file exists.

The next section adds your user directory to the "~/.ddev/nfs_exports.txt" configuration.

Finally, the nssm service is started.

- **run** bash windows_ddev_nfs_setup.sh on the command line to navigate to your Downloads directory

By default, the script allows any directory in your home directory to be shared via NFS. If you want to use a more specific directory (*such as your "sites" directory*), then edit your "~/.ddev/nfs_exports.txt" configuration and change the path. For example:

```
C:\Users\User\sites > /c/Users/User/sites
```

If you changed your "~/.ddev/nfs_exports.txt" file, then restart the winnfsd service via the Services section of the Windows control panel.

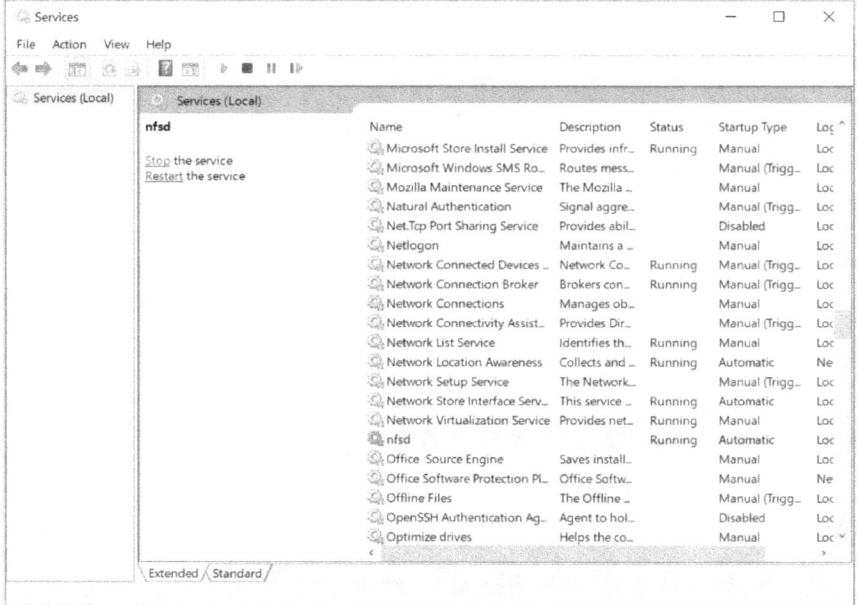

- **update** a DDEV project to use NFS by editing its ".ddev/config.yaml" to to include: `nfs_mount_enabled: true`
- **use** `ddev start` to start your project
- **confirm** NFS mount is working with `ddev debug nfsmount`

You should see something like:

```
$ ddev debug nfsmount
Successfully accessed NFS mount of C:\Users\User\sites\mysite
```

Debugging mount "overlap" issues

In some cases, often if you've used Vagrant or another tool that utilizes NFS mounts, you might end up in an "overlap" situation. This is when your NFS configuration has overlapping directories configured for mounting in either "/etc/exports" (*Mac OS X*) or "~/.ddev/nfs_exports.txt " (*Windows 10*). For example, if your configuration includes both:

```
/Users/michael/sites/acme -alldirs -mapall=501:20 localhost
/Users/michael/sites -alldirs -mapall=501:20 localhost
```

Then this is a case of overlapping mount points, as the first entry is included as part of the second entry. In this example, one possible solution would be to just remove the first entry and then restart the NFS service.

> If you're unable to get NFS mounting working, the official documentation has some useful debugging tips:
>
> https://ddev.readthedocs.io/en/latest/users/performance/#using-nfs-to-mount-the-project-into-the-container

Another useful tool in diagnosing NFS mounting issues is the `ddev debug nfsmount` command. Running this command provides useful technical information to help you debug any potential NFS mounting issues. For example, running this command on a successful mount results in:

```
$ ddev debug nfsmount Successfully accessed NFS mount of
/Users/michael/sites/myproject   TARGET SOURCE FSTYPE
OPTIONS /nfsmount :/Users/michael/sites/myproject nfs
rw,relatime,vers=3,rsize=65536,wsize=65536,namlen=255,hard,n
olock,proto=tcp,timeo=600,retrans=2,sec=sys,mountaddr=192.16
8.65.2,mountvers=3,mountproto=tcp,local_lock=all,addr=192.16
8.65.2 /nfsmount/.ddev
```

The `ddev debug` command also has options for outputting debugging information for docker-compose and DDEV config information.

UTILIZE HTTPS FOR YOUR DDEV-LOCAL PROJECTS

There are many use cases where using *https* is vital to a project's success. In fact, most search engines will rank your site slightly lower in search results if your site isn't served securely. If your site is hosted using *https*, should't also be developed using *https*?

DDEV-Local provides the ability to have all projects served over *https* by default using the popular zero-configuration *mkcert* (`https://github.com/FiloSottile/mkcert`) package. All of the DDEV-Local package installers (*Homebrew, Chocolately, Linuxbrew*) and the Windows 10 installer include *mkcert*.

- **use** `mkcert -install` to install

If you installed DDEV-Local using the Windows 10 installer, you do NOT have to do this step!

> Linux users may require additional steps – see https://ddev.readthedocs.io/en/stable/#linux-mkcert-install-additional-instructions

Once installed, all of your projects will have a primary local URL that uses *https* with no hassle.

ADD FILES TO YOUR PROJECT'S *WEB* CONTAINER'S HOME DIRECTORY

Interested in customizing the *web* container a bit? DDEV provides a ".ddev/homeadditions/" directory whose contents are automatically made available to the DDEV *web* container's home directory. This means that you can automatically include things like Git and SSH settings to a project's *web* container as well as custom Bash settings and scripts.

DDEV provides an example in the ".ddev/homeadditions/" directory, let's review and utilize it.

- **duplicate** the ".ddev/homeadditions/bash_aliases.example" file
- **name** it `.bash_aliases`
- **use** `cat .ddev/homeadditions/.bash_aliases` to view contents (*note the "ll"alias defined*)
- **restart** DDEV
- **use** "ddev ssh" to access the *web* container and utilize the alias
- **type** "ll" and **press** enter to try the alias

WHAT'S NEXT?

This chapter was hopefully a bit of a potpourri of useful information for getting the most out of DDEV-Local. In the next chapter, we'll dive more into an intermediate-level topic – adding an additional service container to a project.

DDEV-LOCAL COMMAND OVERVIEW

Below is a list of DDEV-Local commands we have covered:

1. `help`
2. `version`
3. `composer`
4. `config`
5. `describe`
6. `launch`
7. `restart`

8. start
9. import-db
10. import-files
11. auth
12. pull
13. delete
14. list
15. mysql
16. poweroff
17. pause
18. restore-snapshot
19. sequelpro
20. snapshot
21. ssh
22. stop
23. debug
24. exec
25. export-db
26. hostname

CHAPTER 13.

INTEGRATING APACHE SOLR WITH DRUPAL AND DDEV-LOCAL EXPLAINED

DDEV-Local has the ability to bring in additional services to a project by adding additional Docker containers. The DDEV-Local approach is to use an extra container for each service.

This functionality isn't supported via a project's `ddev config` command or by manually editing the ".ddev/config.yaml" file (*yet*). To integrate an external service container, you will need to use additional Docker Compose files. Why take this approach? Remember, at its heart, DDEV-Local is just a wrapper around Docker Compose.

In this chapter, I'll show you how to add an extra service. We'll use the example of Apache Solr, a popular search server. We'll add Apache Solr to a local Drupal 8 project.

STEP #1. INSTALL THE DRUPAL SEARCH API SOLR MODULE

The Drupal Search API Solr module is dependent on the Search API module, so you'll need to **download** and **install** both modules on your project. For Drupal 8, use Search API Solr version 8.x-3.x or newer.

1. Search API: https://drupal.org/project/search_api
2. Search API Solr: https://drupal.org/project/search_api_solr.

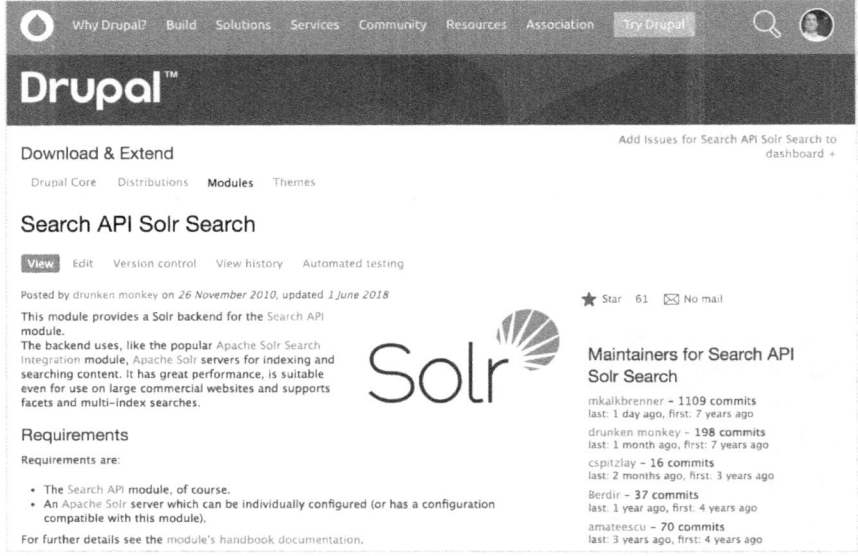

STEP #2. ADD THE DOCKER COMPOSE FILE FOR THE SOLR CONTAINER

DDEV-Local doesn't support adding a Solr service via the ".ddev/config.yaml" file. Rather, you must manually add a "docker-compose.solr.yaml" file to the project's ".ddev/" directory. Luckily the DDEV community provides a starting point.

- **download** the "docker-compose.solr.yaml" file from:

```
https://github.com/drud/ddev/tree/master/pkg/servicetest/testdata/services/docker-compose.solr.yaml.
```

Notable parts of the file include:

1. Line 24 (*of* "docker-compose.solr.yaml"): The "version"

refers to the version of Docker Composer to utilize. This version must be the same as the version that is listed in the project's ".ddev/docker-compose.yaml" file.

2. Line 34: sets the version of Solr to utilize. You can find a list of available versions at:
   `https://hub.docker.com/_/solr/` – it is recommended to use one of the X.Y tags for maximum stability. For example: Drupal 8: 6.6, 7.1, 8.1, 8.2, 8.3

Not sure which version to use? Use the one that matches your project's production environment, or just use the latest.

3. Line 71: defines the name of the "Solr core" that will be available in the container. By default, the name is "dev".

- **download** the "docker-composer.solr.yaml" file
- **place** it in your project's ".ddev/ directory"
- **set** the version of Solr you'd like to use

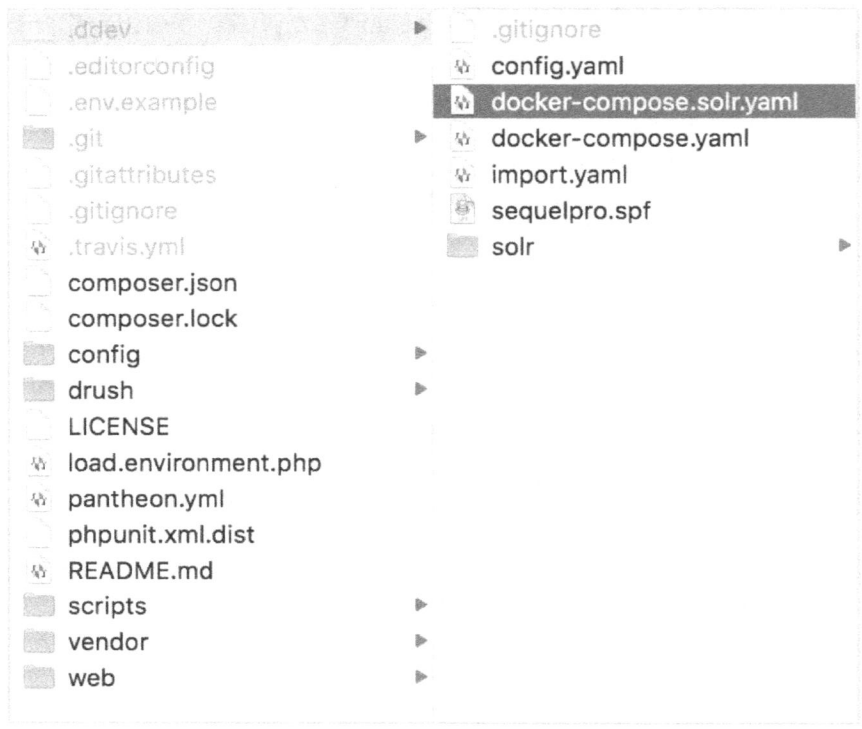

STEP #3. ADD A DDEV-LOCAL COMMAND HOOK

This allows the Search API Solr module to "ping" the Solr service and provide feedback via the Drupal user interface.

- **add** the following code at the bottom of your project's ".ddev/config.yaml" file
- **replace** myproject with your project's name

If your ".ddev/config.yaml" file already has a "hooks" section, then just add the exec command to the existing section.

```
hooks:
post-start:
- exec: curl -s http://myproject.ddev.site:8983/solr/dev/
admin/ping?action=enable -o /dev/null
```

STEP #4. RESTART DDEV AND ENABLE THE MODULES

Restart DDEV (*this will create the new Solr Docker container*) then use Drush or any other method you are comfortable with to enable the Search API Solr Search Defaults module in Drupal 8.

Enabling the Search API Solr Search Defaults module will also enable the Search API and Search API Solr modules. For example, use Drush to enable all three modules:

```
ddev . drush en -y search_api_solr_defaults
```

STEP #5. CREATE A SOLR SERVER DRUPAL CONFIGURATION

The next step is to let Drupal know about the Solr server. This is completed by configuring it via the Drupal user interface:

- **navigate** to /admin/config/search/search-api on your Drupal 8 site
- **click** to edit the "Solr Server" (*created by the Search API Solr Search Defaults module*) with the following values (*anything not listed can be left at its default value*):

    1. Server name: Local Solr Server
    2. Solr Connector: Standard
    3. Solr host: solr
    4. Solr core: dev
    5. Advanced server configuration: solr.install.dir: /opt/solr

▼ CONFIGURE *SOLR* BACKEND

Solr server URI
http://solr:8983/solr/

Solr Connector *
Choose a connector to use for this Solr server.
◉ Standard ←
○ Solr Cloud with Basic Auth
○ Solr Cloud
○ Basic Auth

▼ CONFIGURE *STANDARD* SOLR CONNECTOR

A standard connector usable for local installations of the standard Solr distribution.

HTTP protocol
[http ▼]
The HTTP protocol to use for sending queries.

Solr host *
[solr] ←
The host name or IP of your Solr server, e.g. `localhost` or `www.example.com`.

Solr port *
[8983]
The Jetty example server is at port 8983, while Tomcat uses 8080 by default.

Solr path
[/solr]
The path that identifies the Solr instance to use on the server.

Solr core
[dev] ←
The name that identifies the Solr core to use on the server.

Query timeout *
[5]
The timeout in seconds for search queries sent to the Solr server.

STEP #6. INSTALL THE SOLR CONFIGURATION FILES

Solr require configuration files installed in order to operate. The configuration files are dependent on the version of Solr being used. The Drupal Search API Solr module (*8.x-3.x*) provides a mechanism to generate these configuration files.

Once the Drupal Solr configuration is created,

- **click** the "View" tab of the Local Solr config
- **click** "Get config.zip" button to download the generated Solr configuration files

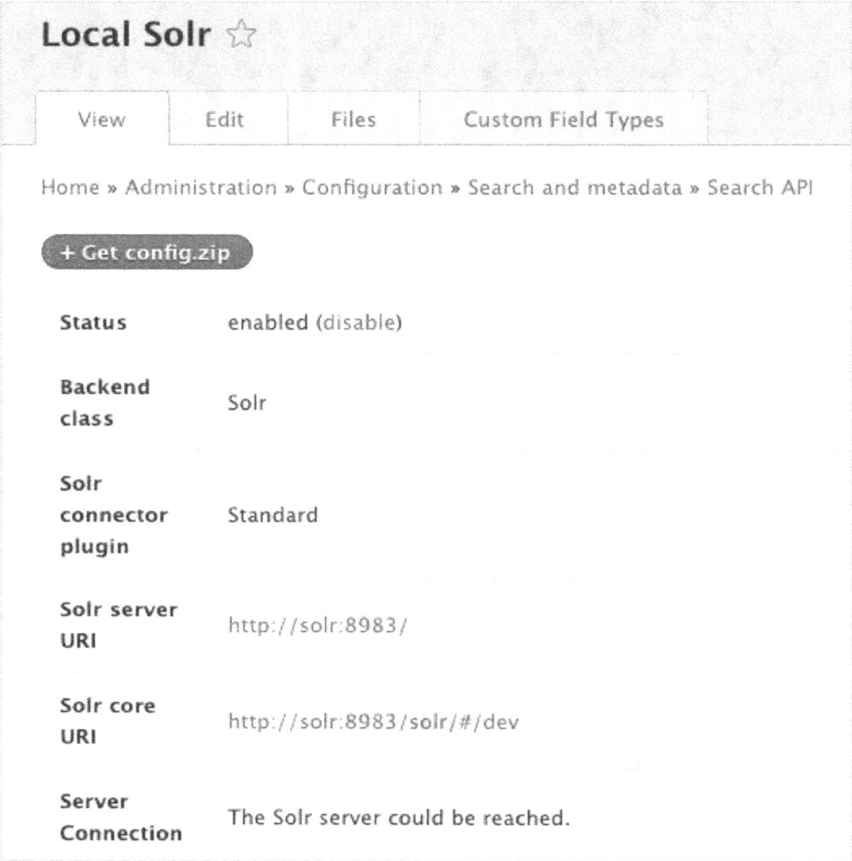
Local Solr
View
Edit
Files
Custom Field Types
Home » Administration » Configuration » Search and metadata » Search API
+ Get config.zip
Status
enabled (disable)
Backend class
Solr
Solr connector plugin
Standard
Solr server URI
http://solr:8983/
Solr core URI
http://solr:8983/solr/#/dev
Server Connection
The Solr server could be reached.

- **extract** the files
- **move** files to your project's ".ddev/solr/conf/" directory

composer.json
composer.lock
config
drush
LICENSE
load.environment.php
pantheon.yml
phpunit.xml.dist
README.md
scripts
vendor
web
config.yaml
docker-compose.solr.yaml
docker-compose.yaml
import.yaml
sequelpro.spf
solr
conf
elevate.xml
mapping-ISO...in1Accent.txt
protwords.txt
schema_extra_fields.xml
schema_extra_types.xml
schema.xml
solrconfig_extra.xml
solrconfig_spellcheck.xml
solrconfig.xml
solrcore.properties
stopwords.txt
synonyms.txt

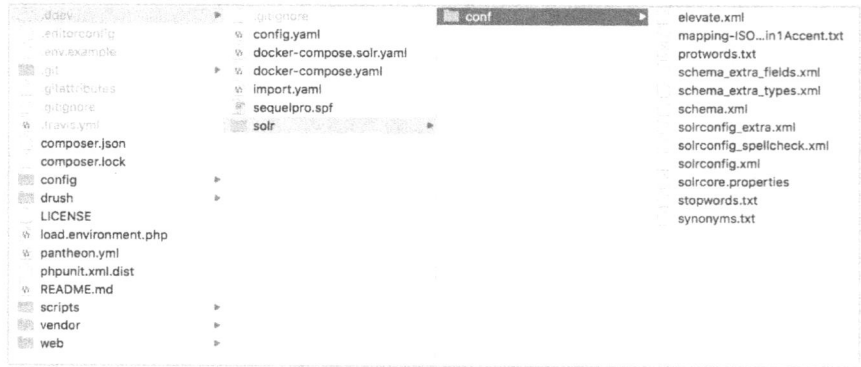

> NOTE: line 60 of the "docker-composer.solr.yaml" file mounts the ".ddev/solr/" directory ("./solr") on the Solr server, making the configuration files available to the server – cool!

STEP #7. REBUILD THE SOLR CONTAINER AND RESTART YOUR DDEV-LOCAL PROJECT

Once the Solr configuration files are in-place, the Solr container's data must be rebuilt.

- **remove** the Docker volume that contains the Solr data
- **replace** "myproject" with the name of your project
- **restart** the project (*which recreates the Docker volume using the newly installed Solr configuration files*).

From the command line it looks like the following:

```
$ ddev stop
$ docker volume rm ddev-myproject_solrdata
$ ddev start
```

Once DDEV has restarted,

- **go to** your Search API configuration page ("/admin/config/search/search-api")
- **click** the "Local Solr Server" link

If all is working, then the page should report that the Solr server and core can be accessed!

Default Solr server created by the Solr Search Defaults module	
Status	enabled (disable)
Backend class	Solr
Search indexes	Default Solr content index
Solr connector plugin	Standard
Solr server URI	http://solr:8983/
Solr core URI	http://solr:8983/solr/#/dev
Server Connection	The Solr server could be reached.
Core Connection	The Solr core could be accessed (latency: 4.1788087615967 ms).
Configured Solr Version	8.3.1
Detected Solr Version	8.3.1

STEP #8. CLEAN-UP AND INDEXING

Once the Solr server is up-and-running,

- **disable** the Search API Solr Search Defaults module

Refer to the Search API module documentation for information about creating a search index for your Solr server.

ADDING OTHER SERVICES TO DDEV-LOCAL

You can find official documentation about adding additional services to DDEV-Local at:

> https://ddev.readthedocs.io/en/latest/users/extend/additional-services/

WHAT'S NEXT?

In this chapter, we really started to take advantage of DDEV-Local's Docker underpinnings by adding a custom service container. In the next chapter, we'll learn how we can extend the default DDEV-Local *web* container using a Dockerfile.

DDEV-LOCAL COMMAND OVERVIEW

Below is a list of DDEV-Local commands we have covered:

1. `help`
2. `version`
3. `composer`
4. `config`
5. `describe`
6. `launch`
7. `restart`
8. `start`
9. `import-db`
10. `import-files`
11. `auth`
12. `pull`
13. `delete`
14. `list`
15. `mysql`
16. `poweroff`
17. `pause`
18. `restore-snapshot`
19. `sequelpro`

20. snapshot
21. ssh
22. stop
23. debug
24. exec
25. export-db
26. hostname

CHAPTER 14.

EXTENDING DDEV-LOCAL'S WEB CONTAINER EXPLAINED

Sometimes it is necessary to be able to use additional tools when developing your project that aren't included in the default DDEV-Local container configuration. This is often the situation when it comes to tools commonly used by front-end developers. There are a few ways to extend what is provided by the DDEV-Local containers including:

1. Adding additional (*Debian*) packages directly to the *web* container using the webimage_extra_packages configuration parameter in ".ddev/config.yml".

    - Pros: easy solution.
    - Cons: often includes a post-start command in order to complete installation of packages, which must be run every time a project is started.

2. Defining a new container dedicated to the front-end tools (*see* https://bit.ly/ddev-sass-watch *for an example*).

    - Pros: most flexible solution.
    - Cons: requires more Docker (*Docker Compose, specifically*) knowledge.

3. Adding additional (*Debian*) packages to the web container by extending it via a Dockerfile.

    ◦ Pros: fairly easy solution, package installation only performed when the Docker image is built.

    ◦ Cons: using this method overrides any packages added via the *webimage_extra_packages* configuration variable.

In this section, we will take the third approach to modify the *web* container in a few different examples:

1. Addition of Ruby and Compass
2. Modifying the minimum TLS version
3. Addition of *Node.js*

> **Note**: there has been some discussion about nvm and possibly other tools being automatically included in the DDEV-Local web container by default in a future version. See https://github.com/drud/ddev/issues/2380

Before we get to the examples, let's cover some of the basics.

WHAT IS A DOCKERFILE?

A Dockerfile is the instructions used by Docker to build a Docker container. DDEV-Local provides Docker images for the *web*, *db*, and *dba* containers, but also provides a mechanism for developers to extend each container by looking for additional Dockerfiles in ".ddev/web-build/ and .ddev/db-build/' (*DDEV-Local does not allow the dba container to be modified*).

DDEV-LOCAL AND DOCKERFILES

One of the features of Docker is that it allows for Dockerfiles to extend other Dockerfiles in a very concise manner. In the case of the *web* container, DDEV-Local takes advantage of this by first looking for a ".ddev/web-build/Dockerfile". If it finds one, it adds those additional instructions on top of the default image building instructions.

Example 1: Extending the web container Dockerfile with Ruby and Compass

Let's look at the example of adding Sass and Compass Ruby gems to the web container. This is a multi-step process:

1. Extend the default DDEV-Local *web* container.
2. Add the *rubygems, ruby-full,* and *build-essential* packages to the web container.
3. Use *gem install* to install all of the necessary gems.

Let's get started:

- **create** a new, empty ".ddev/web-build/Dockerfile" (*this should be an empty text file with no file extension*)
- **add** the following to the top of the new file

```
ARG BASE_IMAGE
FROM $BASE_IMAGE
```

These two lines inherit the DDEV-Local default *web* container as a starting point.

- **add** the following:

```
RUN apt-get update && DEBIAN_FRONTEND=noninteractive
apt-get install -y -o Dpkg::Options::="--force-confold"
```

```
      --no-install-recommends --no-install-suggests
      build-essential ruby-full rubygems
```

Please note that there is only one line of code, beginning with the RUN command. Due to formatting, some lines may be wrapped.

This line of code does the same thing as adding webimage_extra_packages to your project's ".ddev/config.yaml" file. It adds the *rubygems, ruby-full,* and *build-essential* packages to the *web* container using apt-get (*a very common command-line tool for managing packages in Linux*).

Previously we installed the *rubygems* package, now the *web* container has the ability to use the *gem install* command to download and install the front-end Ruby gems necessary for the project. The last line of the Dockerfile installs Compass as well as some additional commonly-used front-end development gems.

```
      RUN gem install compass compass-normalize compass-rgbapng
      toolkit breakpoint singularitygs susy sass-globbing
```

The complete Dockerfile is then:

```
ARG BASE_IMAGE
FROM $BASE_IMAGE
RUN apt-get update && DEBIAN_FRONTEND=noninteractive
apt-get install -y -o Dpkg::Options::="--force-confold"
--no-install-recommends --no-install-suggests
build-essential ruby-full rubygems
RUN gem install compass compass-normalize compass-rgbapng
toolkit breakpoint singularitygs susy sass-globbing
```

Again, note that there are only four lines of code, each beginning with a capitalized command. Due to formatting, some lines may be wrapped.

Once the ".ddev/web-build/Dockerfile" is saved,

- **run** ddev start to create the updated *web* image and start a new container based on it

To test the new front-end functionality,

- **ensure** you have a theme directory in your project that contains a "/sass/" or "/scss/" directory
- **use** ddev ssh to connect to the *web* container
- **navigate** into the theme directory
- **run** compass compile

You should see a successful compilation of your Sass files!

```
$ compass compile
modified config.rb
clean css
delete css/myproject.normalize.css
delete css/myproject.normalize.css.map
delete css/myproject.print.css
delete css/myproject.print.css.map
delete css/myproject.styles.css
delete css/myproject.styles.css.map
write css/myproject.normalize.css
write css/myproject.normalize.css.map
write css/myproject.print.css
write css/myproject.print.css.map
write css/myproject.styles.css
write css/myproject.styles.css.map
```

Example 2: Extending the web container Dockerfile with an old TLS version

In this example, we'll modify the minimum TLS version for the DDEV-Local *web* container. By default, the *web* container supports TLS 1.2. In some situations your project may be trying to access remote servers that use an older (*and insecure!*) TLS protocol. While the recommended solution is to update the version of TLS used by the remote server, sometimes this is not possible.

- **create** a new, empty ".ddev/web-build/Dockerfile" (*this should be an empty text file with no file extension*)
- **add** the following to the top of the new file to extend the default DDEV-Local web container Dockerfile

```
ARG BASE_IMAGE
FROM $BASE_IMAGE
```

Next, we will use *sed* to substitute "1.0" for "1.2" in the appropriate configuration file in order to modify the web container's minimum TLS version. *sed* is a text editor without a user interface commonly used in Linux environments.

- **add** the following to the Dockerfile

```
RUN sed -i 's/TLSv1.2/TLSv1.0/g' /etc/ssl/openssl.cnf
```

The complete Dockerfile looks like the following:

```
ARG BASE_IMAGE
FROM $BASE_IMAGE
RUN sed -i 's/TLSv1.2/TLSv1.0/g' /etc/ssl/openssl.cnf
```

Again, note that there are only three lines of code, each beginning with a capitalized command. Due to formatting, some lines may be wrapped.

Once the ".ddev/web-build/Dockerfile" is saved,

- **run** ddev start to create the updated *web* image and start a new container based on it
- **run the following command to confirm the**

new minimum TLS version is in use

```
ddev . cat /etc/ssl/openssl.cnf | grep TLS
```

This will return the `MinProtocol` supported:

```
MinProtocol = TLSv1.0
```

Example 3: Extending the web container Dockerfile with Node.js

In this example, we'll modify the DDEV-Local *web* container by adding Node.js, a commonly used tool for front-end development.

- **create** a new, empty Dockerfile: ".ddev/web-build/Dockerfile" (*this should be an empty text file with no file extension*)
- **add** the following to the top of the new file to extend the default DDEV-Local *web* container Dockerfile

```
ARG BASE_IMAGE
FROM $BASE_IMAGE
```

Next, we will install and use nvm to install Node.js. *nvm*, Node Version Manager, is a tool that is used to install a specific version of Node.js. First, we'll specify a couple of configuration settings including the exact version of Node.js that is required for the project.

- **add** the following to the Dockerfile

```
ENV NVM_DIR=/usr/local/nvm
ENV NODE_DEFAULT_VERSION=v12.18.3
```

- **download** and **run** the *nvm* install script
- **install** the specified version of Node.js

The commands should look like the following:

```
RUN curl -sL https://raw.githubusercontent.com/nvm-sh/nvm/v0.35.3/install.sh -o install_nvm.sh
RUN mkdir -p $NVM_DIR && bash install_nvm.sh
RUN echo "source $NVM_DIR/nvm.sh" >>/etc/profile
RUN bash -ic "nvm install $NODE_DEFAULT_VERSION && nvm use $NODE_DEFAULT_VERSION"
RUN chmod -R ugo+w $NVM_DIR
```

The complete Dockerfile looks like the following:

```
ARG BASE_IMAGE
FROM $BASE_IMAGE
ENV NVM_DIR=/usr/local/nvm
ENV NODE_DEFAULT_VERSION=v12.18.3
RUN curl -sL https://raw.githubusercontent.com/nvm-sh/nvm/v0.35.3/install.sh -o install_nvm.sh
RUN mkdir -p $NVM_DIR && bash install_nvm.sh
RUN echo "source $NVM_DIR/nvm.sh" >>/etc/profile
RUN bash -ic "nvm install $NODE_DEFAULT_VERSION && nvm use $NODE_DEFAULT_VERSION"
RUN chmod -R ugo+w $NVM_DIR
```

Again, note that there are only nine lines of code, each beginning with a capitalized command. Due to formatting, some lines may be wrapped.

Once the ".ddev/web-build/Dockerfile" is saved,

- **run** ddev start to create the updated *web* image and start a new container based on it

To confirm that Node.js is installed and ready to use,

- **run** the following and confirm the version

```
$ ddev . node --version
v12.18.3
```

SUMMARY

While the examples in the chapter focused on the DDEV-Local *web* container, remember that this technique can be used to also extend the DDEV-Local *db* container by creating a Dockerfile in the ".ddev/db-build/" directory.

WHAT'S NEXT?

In this chapter, we continued to learn how we can extend the default capabilities of DDEV-Local. In the next chapter, we'll learn how we can provide a quick glimpse of our local site via a public url using the "ddev share" command.

DDEV-LOCAL COMMAND OVERVIEW

Below is a list of DDEV-Local commands we have covered:

1. `help`
2. `version`
3. `composer`
4. `config`
5. `describe`
6. `launch`
7. `restart`
8. `start`
9. `import-db`

10. import-files
11. auth
12. pull
13. delete
14. list
15. mysql
16. poweroff
17. pause
18. restore-snapshot
19. sequelpro
20. snapshot
21. ssh
22. stop
23. debug
24. exec
25. export-db
26. hostname

CHAPTER 15.

SHARE YOUR DDEV-LOCAL PROJECT ONLINE EXPLAINED

Version 1.9.0 of DDEV-local introduced the ability to share your local project online via a temporary, public URL using *ngrok* (https://ngrok.com/).

This allows you the ability to quickly and securely provide access to your local site to other developers and stakeholders as well as an easy way to test your local site on other devices.

> *ngrok* is a service that exposes local servers behind NATs and firewalls via public URLs over secure tunnels.

Once the small *ngrok* client is installed on your local machine, the `ddev share` command will enable the sharing and provide you with a public URL for your local site.

While there are paid tiers for the *ngrok* service, a free tier is provided with reasonable limits on usage. See the *ngrok* web site for details. In the first example, we'll utilize the free, anonymous tier.

The free, anonymous tier does NOT encrypt your data between

your local and the *ngrok* servers, even though an *https* connection is provided from the *ngrok* servers to connected clients. Therefore, it is strongly suggested that once you get the free, anonymous tier working, create a free account and authenticate your local *ngrok* client to ensure your data is encrypted the entire trip.

> **Note**: This is a one-time setup for your machine, and does not have to be repeated for each of your DDEV-Local projects.

STEP 1: INSTALL THE NGROK CLIENT

- **download** ngrok client specific to your OS from https://ngrok.com/download

While there are instructions to download and install ngrok on various operating systems, I found that using Homebrew (*Mac OS X and Linux*) was easiest.

- **use** brew cask install ngrok

If you're using Windows 10 and Chocolately,

- **use** choco install ngrok

STEP 2: SHARING YOUR LOCAL SITE

- **run** ddev share

If successful, this command will return some information about the share, including public URLs with which you can access the site.

As requests are made to the site, the screen will update detailing each request.

```
ngrok by @inconshreveable                                          (Ctrl+C to quit)

Session Status                online
Session Expires               7 hours, 56 minutes
Version                       2.3.30
Region                        United States (us)
Web Interface                 http://127.0.0.1:4040
Forwarding                    http://94d5c548.ngrok.io -> http://127.0.0.1:32786
Forwarding                    https://94d5c548.ngrok.io -> http://127.0.0.1:32786

Connections                   ttl     opn     rt1     rt5     p50     p90
                              6       0       0.02    0.01    4.99    8.92

HTTP Requests
-------------

GET /sites/default/files/favicons/favicon-16x16.png                 200 OK
GET /sites/default/files/favicons/favicon-32x32.png                 200 OK
GET /sites/default/files/inline-images/project_coaching.png         200 OK
GET /themes/de8/images/DrupalEasy_logo_small.png                    200 OK
GET /themes/de8/fontello/font/drupaleasy.woff2                      200 OK
GET /modules/contrib/eu_cookie_compliance/js/eu_cookie_compliance.js 200 OK
GET /core/assets/vendor/jquery.cookie/jquery.cookie.min.js          200 OK
GET /themes/de8/bootstrap/assets/javascripts/bootstrap/transition.js 200 OK
GET /themes/de8/bootstrap/assets/javascripts/bootstrap/tab.js       200 OK
GET /themes/de8/bootstrap/assets/javascripts/bootstrap/scrollspy.js 200 OK
```

> **Note**: The `https://94d5c548.ngrok.io` public URL is forwarding the insecure `http://127.0.0.1:32786`. If we were to set up a *ngrok* account and authenticate our local *ngrok* client, it would be forwarding `https://127.0.0.1:32786` instead. Use Crtl-C to stop the sharing.

ADDITIONAL NGROK FEATURES AND FUNCTIONALITY

Secure your data by signing up for a free *ngrok* account and then authenticating your local *ngrok* client with your account credentials using the command provided by the *ngrok* web site:

```
./ngrok authtoken
<a-long-string-of-characters-that-is-your-token>
```

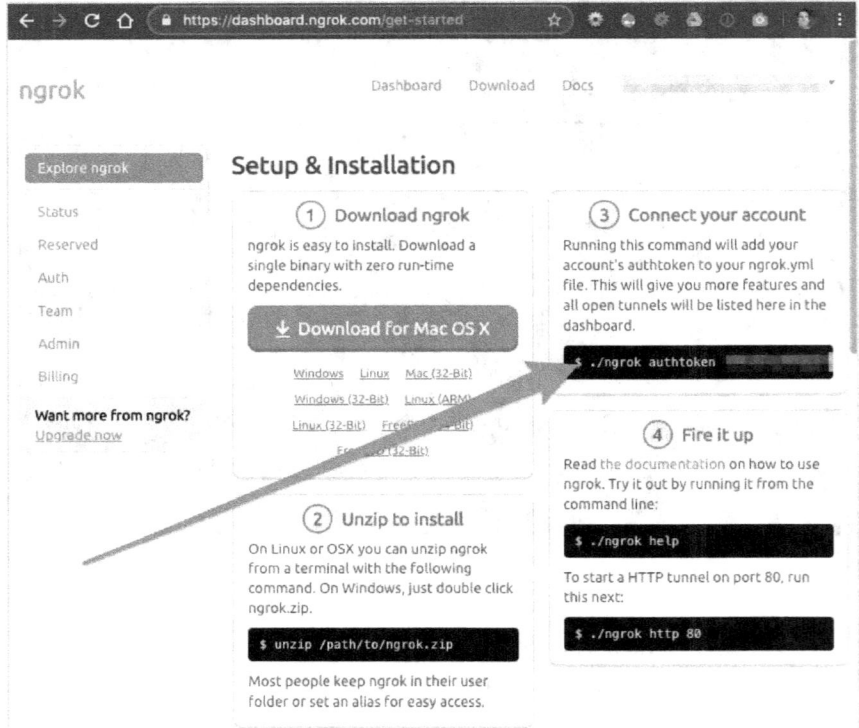

Once your local *ngrok* client is authenticated, the next time you do a `ddev share`, you'll be able to see that your connection uses *https* from end-to-end.

While the free *ngrok* plan is normally sufficient for smaller projects, paid *ngrok* plans include multiple users, custom domains and subdomains, additional connections, static IP addresses, and other features.

WHAT'S NEXT?

In this chapter, we learned how to share our local site with other members of the development team. In the next chapter, we'll tackle another topic that is typically challenging with an old-school AMP stack: setting up and using Xdebug.

DDEV-LOCAL COMMAND OVERVIEW

Below is a list of DDEV-Local commands we have covered:

1. `help`
2. `version`
3. `composer`
4. `config`
5. `describe`
6. `launch`
7. `restart`
8. `start`
9. `import-db`
10. `import-files`
11. `auth`
12. `pull`
13. `delete`
14. `list`
15. `mysql`
16. `poweroff`
17. `pause`
18. `restore-snapshot`
19. `sequelpro`
20. `snapshot`

21. ssh
22. stop
23. debug
24. exec
25. export-db
26. hostname
27. share

CHAPTER 16.

USING DDEV-LOCAL WITH XDEBUG AND PHPSTORM EXPLAINED

In the last chapter, we saw how to add a search server to DDEV-Local.

In this chapter, we'll continue to integrate DDEV-Local with other resources, Xdebug and PhpStorm.

1. *Xdebug* is a powerful debugging tool that allows developers to set breakpoints, inspect variables, and step through code when developing code or tracking bugs: `https://xdebug.org`.
2. *PhpStorm* is a very commonly-used integrated development environment (IDE): `https://jetbrains.com/phpstorm`.

There are three steps we'll need to make this integration work:

1. Configure the DDEV-Local project for Xdebug.
2. Configure the PhpStorm project for Xdebug.
3. Configure the web browser for Xdebug.

STEP #1. CONFIGURE THE DDEV-LOCAL PROJECT FOR XDEBUG

DDEV-Local's default project configuration has Xdebug functionality disabled by default. Luckily, it is dead-simple to enable and disable via the following commands:

```
ddev xdebug on ddev xdebug off
```

You can also enable/disable Xdebug via a setting in the project's ".ddev/config.yaml" file.

- **open** the file for editing
- **change** the `xdebug_enabled` setting from `false` to `true`
- **restart** DDEV-Local for the project

Note the name of my project in this example is *drupal8*, which is also the type of project.

```
APIVersion: v1.1.0
name: drupal8
type: drupal8
docroot: web
php_version: "7.1"
router_http_port: "80"
router_https_port: "443"
xdebug_enabled: true
additional_hostnames: []
additional_fqdns: []
provider: default
```

Once the configuration change is made, when restarting DDEV-Local, you'll see the *web* container being recreated with Xdebug is now enabled.

```
Michaels-MacBook-Pro:drupal8 michael$ ddev restart
Restarting project drupal8...
Stopping ddev-drupal8-web ... done
```

```
Stopping ddev-drupal8-dba ... done
Stopping ddev-drupal8-db ... done Stopping ddev-router ...
done
Removing ddev-router ... done
Network ddev_default is external, skipping
Starting ddev-drupal8-db ... done
Starting ddev-drupal8-dba ... done
Recreating ddev-drupal8-web ... done Network ddev_default
is external, skipping
Creating ddev-router ... done Ensuring write permissions
for drupal8
Successfully restarted drupal8
Your project can be reached at http://drupal8.ddev.site,
https://drupal8.ddev.site, http://127.0.0.1:32780
```

It is important to note that the performance of the site will take a bit of a hit when Xdebug is enabled. It is recommended to only have it enabled when you are actively using it, otherwise, set it to `xdebug_enabled: false` (*be sure to* `ddev restart` *whenever you change it*).

STEP #2. CONFIGURE THE PHPSTORM PROJECT FOR XDEBUG.

Setting up PhpStorm to work with Xdebug requires that we configure PhpStorm to look for the Xdebug information coming out of the web server as PHP code is processed. PhpStorm must know where to look for this information. Once this connection is established, then PhpStorm can issue commands via Xdebug to the web server to pause/unpause execution of the code by the web server, as well as inspect PHP variables, and other debugging functionality.

The following steps assume that you already have the project open in PhpStorm.

- **open** PhpStorm's preferences
- **navigate** to the *Languages & Frameworks* section, then *PHP*,

then *Servers*

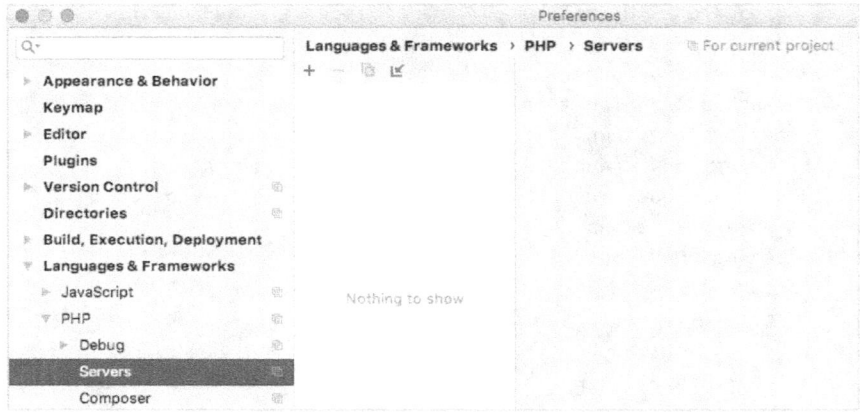

- **click** the "+" button to add a new *Server*
- **edit** the following:
  - "Name =" the name of your DDEV-Local project (*typically the same as the project directory name. In this example, I'll use "drupal8".*)
  - "Host =" the URL you use to access the site on your local environment (`drupal8.ddev.site`)
  - "Port: 80" (*default*).
  - "Debugger: Xdebug" (*default*)
- **check** the box to *Use path mappings*
- **map** the absolute path to your project root in the host operating system (*in my example* "/Users/michael/sites/drupal8") to /var/www/html – this is the absolute path to the codebase in the default DDEV-Local *web* container. This allows Xdebug to sync up what is happening in the browser with the specific line of code in the codebase

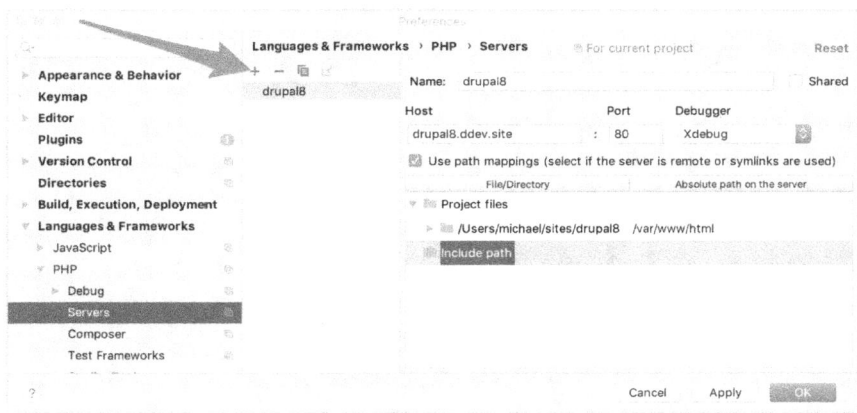

STEP #3. CONFIGURE THE WEB BROWSER FOR XDEBUG

This example will utilize Google Chrome, but the steps are almost identical for other modern browsers.

So far, we've configured the DDEV-Local web server container to provide Xdebug information as well as PhpStorm to receive the information. The missing piece is a *switch* to tell the web browser that we want the web server to provide the debugging information for a particular page request. This is accomplished via the Xdebug Helper browser extension.

JetBrains, the maker of PhpStorm, provides Xdebug Helper. You can download and install it for various browsers from:

> https://confluence.jetbrains.com/display/PhpStorm/
> Browser+Debugging+Extensions.

Once installed and enabled in a web browser, it appears as a small *bug* icon in the browser's toolbar:

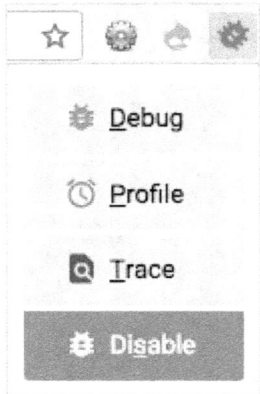

In this example, we'll just focus on the *Debug* and *Disable* settings. When you want the web server to provide debugging information, select *Debug*, otherwise leave it set to *Disable* (*debugging requires extra horsepower, so it is best to leave it disabled unless you are actively using it*).

- **right-click** the bug icon
- **select** "Options"
- **set** the *IDE Key* to *PhpStorm*
- **click** to save

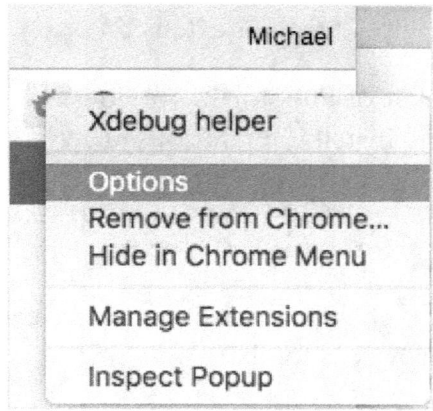

IDE key

Select your IDE to use the default sessionkey or choose other to use a custom key.

[PhpStorm ▼]   PHPSTORM   Save

STEP #4. DEBUG SOMETHING!

With the configuration complete, it's time to debug some code. There are 4 steps:

1. Set a breakpoint
2. Enable *listening* in PhpStorm
3. Enable *Debug* in the web browser
4. Load a page

#1. Set a breakpoint

In this example, we'll set a breakpoint (*a place where we will stop code execution so that we can inspect some PHP variables*) on line 20 of Drupal 8's "index.php" file.

To set a breakpoint in PhpStorm,

- **open** the file
- **click** to the right of the line number

A red circle will appear, indicating a breakpoint has been set. Simply click the breakpoint again to remove it.

```
index.php
 1      <?php
 2
 3      /** @file ...*/
10
11      use ...
13
14      $autoloader = require_once 'autoload.php';
15
16      $kernel = new DrupalKernel('prod', $autoloader);
17
18      $request = Request::createFromGlobals();
19      $response = $kernel->handle($request);
20   ●  $response->send();
21
22      $kernel->terminate($request, $response);
23
```

#2. Enable *listening* in PhpStorm

Similar to how the browser extension tells the web server when to provide debugging information, we must also tell PhpStorm to *listen* for debugging information. This is done via an icon in the PhpStorm toolbar. The icon includes an old-school telephone handset and bug images.

When the icon includes a red circle with a line through it, it is NOT listening.

When the icon includes sound waves coming out of the old-school telephone handset, it IS listening.

#3. Enable *Debug* in the web browser

As mentioned in the previous section, just **click** the *Debug* option in the Xdebug helper, so that the bug turns green.

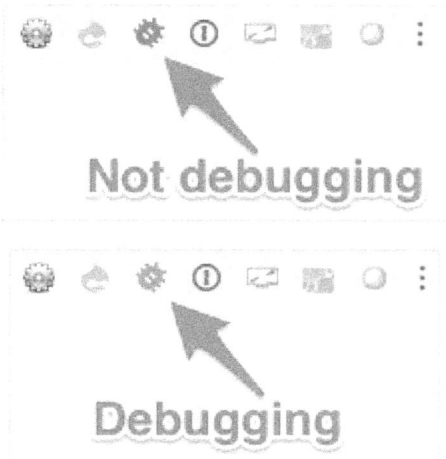

#4. Load a page

At this point, everything should be considered, so the next step is to just load the home page of the site. If everything is configured properly three things will happen:

1. The PhpStorm *Debugger* tab should open.
2. The code execution should pause at the breakpoint.
3. The *Variables* pane should display a list of all the current PHP variables and their values.

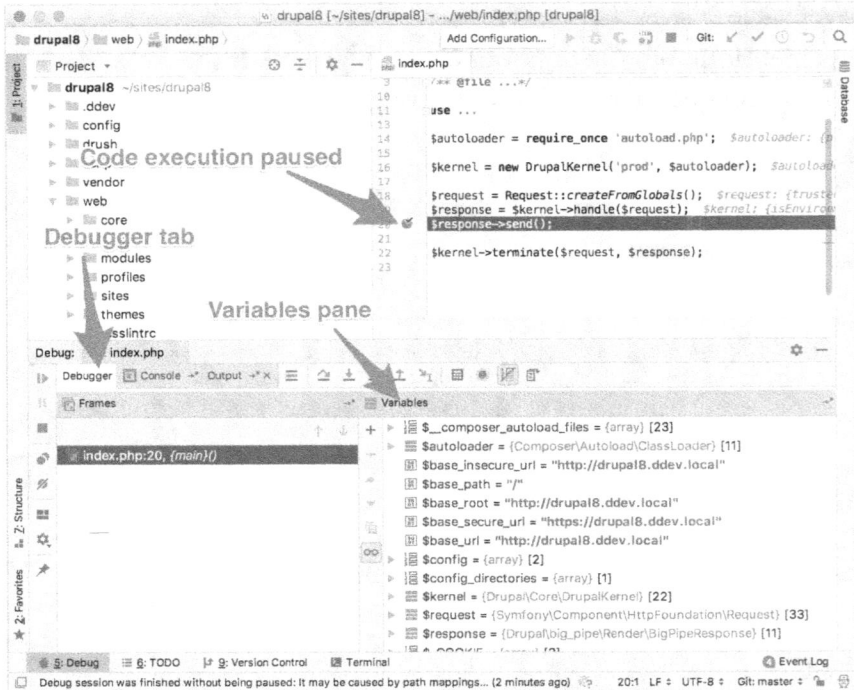

At this point, various code execution controls are available to the developer, including (*but definitely not limited to*):

1. Resume program – resumes execution of the code.

2. Stop – stops execution of the code, debugging session ends.

3. Step over – moves the code execution forward one line, without stepping into any functions or methods.

4. Step into – moves the code execution forward one line, including stepping into any functions or methods.

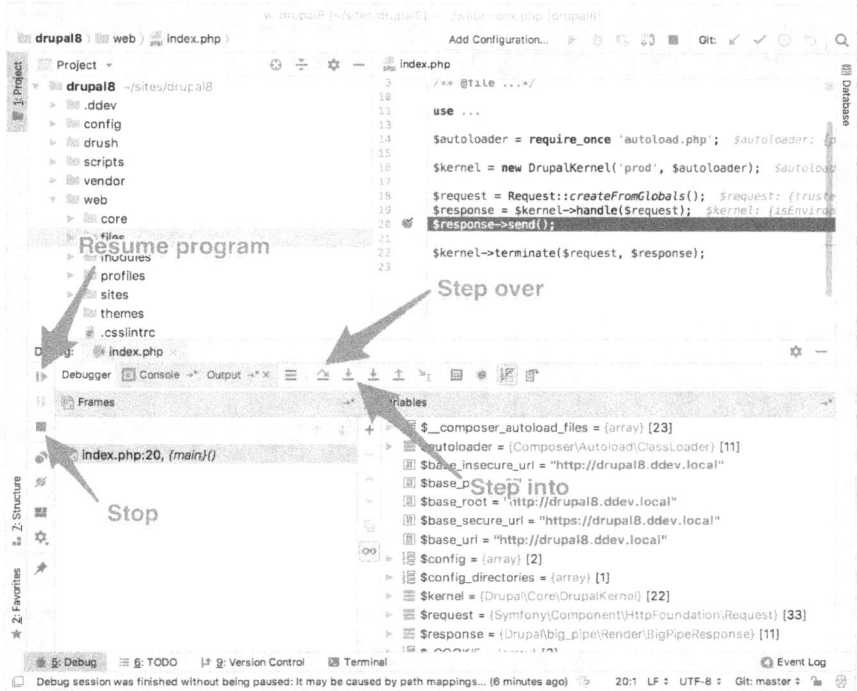

The full functionality of using PhpStorm's debugging tools is beyond the scope of this book, but being able to set breakpoints and inspect variables are basic skills that all Xdebug users take advantage of.

DEBUGGING FROM THE COMMAND-LINE

As a developer, sometimes it is necessary to debug from the command-line, instead of a web browser. When developing a Drupal site, for example, it is useful to be able to debug things like custom Drush commands as well as custom migrations run with Drush commands.

In order to debug command-line commands, from the command-line,

- **use** ddev ssh to connect to the DDEV-Local *web* container

Starting with version 1.15.0, DDEV-Local automatically sets the *PHP_IDE_CONFIG* environment variable. This variable is used by PhpStorm to determine which path mapping configuration should be used. For example, if `myproject` is the name of your DDEV-Local project (*typically the same as the project directory name*) then, it will be set as follows:

```
PHP_IDE_CONFIG="serverName=myproject.ddev.site"
```

- **set** your breakpoint(s)
- **click** the icon with the old-school telephone handset to *Start Listening for PHP Debug Connections*
- **run** the selected command

If you're running a Drush command, be sure you're running the version of Drush installed in your project, not the version pre-installed in the DDEV *web* container. This usually means you'll want to do something like this from "/var/www/html/web" directory within the *web* container:

```
../vendor/bin/drush cr
```

This will directly call the version of Drush installed in the project root (*/var/www/html*), and NOT the version of Drush installed globally in the DDEV-Local *web* container.

The DDEV-Local default *web* container includes a number of commonly-used, command-line tools often used by open source developers, including:

1. `Drush`
2. `WP-CLI`
3. `Composer`

All are located in "/usr/local/bin/".

ENDING YOUR DEBUGGING SESSION

As has been noted several times in this chapter, there is a not-insignificant performance hit when debugging is enabled. Therefore, it is important to disable Xdebug when the debugging session is complete.

- **disable** *listening* in PhpStorm
- **disable** the Xdebug Helper in your browser
- **set** xdebug_enabled: false
- **run** ddev restart

USING THE DDEV-LOCAL "LOGS" COMMAND FOR DEBUGGING

DDEV-Local also provides a `logs` command to easily access logs from DDEV-Local managed project containers. Without any flags, the following command provides a list of logs from the *web* container:

    ddev logs

To see logs from the database container,

- **use** ddev logs -service db

To follow the logs from the *web* container in real time,

- **use** ddev logs -follow

To return to the command prompt,

- **use** Crtl-c

There is also a `--tail` flag for showing a specific number of lines from the log and a `--time` flag for adding timestamps to each line. For example, to show the last 10 lines from the *db* container logs with a timestamp, use:

```
ddev logs --service=db --tail=10 --time
```

WHAT'S NEXT?

In this chapter, you learned how to set up and utilize Xdebug with the PhpStorm IDE. You also learned how DDEV-Local provides access to service log files. In the next chapter, we'll talk a little bit about where you can go from here!

DDEV-LOCAL COMMAND OVERVIEW

Below is a list of DDEV-Local commands we have covered:

1. `help`
2. `version`
3. `composer`
4. `config`
5. `describe`
6. `launch`
7. `restart`
8. `start`
9. `import-db`
10. `import-files`
11. `auth`
12. `pull`

13. `delete`
14. `list`
15. `mysql`
16. `poweroff`
17. `pause`
18. `restore-snapshot`
19. `sequelpro`
20. `snapshot`
21. `ssh`
22. `stop`
23. `debug`
24. `exec`
25. `export-db`
26. `hostname`
27. `share`
28. `logs`
29. `xdebug`

CHAPTER 17.

WHAT'S NEXT?

Congratulations! You've reached the end of *Local Web Development with DDEV Explained*. Hopefully I've convinced you that DDEV-Local is a great option for your local development work.

SO WHAT COMES NEXT?

If you ever find yourself needing additional help, or curious about new functionality in DDEV-Local, there are several official channels to be aware of:

1. Interactive command-line help – this is useful if you are looking for a specific command, or additional information on a specific command. Use the `-h` flag to see additional help. For example:
    1. `ddev -h` will display a list of all DDEV-Local available commands.
    2. `ddev import-db -h` will display a list of flags that you can use with the `import-db` command
2. You can find the official DDEV-Local documentation at `https://ddev.readthedocs.io/`.
3. The #ddev channel on the Drupal community Slack

provides interactive chat with other DDEV-Local users, and usually DDEV-Local team members: `https://www.drupal.org/slack`.

4. The DDEV-Local team encourages the use of the "ddev" tag on Stackoverflow. Many commonly-asked questions are asked and answered here: `https://stackoverflow.com/tags/ddev`.

5. You can use the DDEV-Local development issue queue to search for known issues and to file bug reports or feature requests: `https://github.com/drud/ddev/issues`. This is a great resource if you've encountered a bug or are interested in suggesting a new feature for DDEV-Local. Be sure to search the issue queue before posting to ensure that someone else hasn't already opened an issue on the same topic.

I hope to see you around in the community, and wish you all the best in your use of DDEV-Local!

APPENDIX

PACKAGES INSTALLED IN DDEV DEFAULT CONTAINERS

WEB CONTAINER

The following is a partial list of packages installed in the default *web* (*Debian GNU/Linux*) container of a DDEV-Local project. For a full list of packages installed (*and version numbers*), **run** `dpkg-query -l` from inside the container.

- apache2 – Apache HTTP Server
- apt – Command line package manager
- bash – GNU Bourne Again SHell
- blackfire.io – PHP code performance tool
- bzip2 – High-quality block-sorting file compressor
- ca-certificates – Common CA certificates
- curl – Command line tool for transferring data with URL syntax
- diffutils – File comparison utilities
- findutils – Utilities for finding files–find, xargs
- git – Version control system
- grep – GNU grep, egrep and fgrep

- gzip – GNU compression utilities
- imagemagick – Image manipulation programs
- less – Pager program similar to more
- mawk – A pattern scanning and text processing language
- mime-support – MIME files 'mime.types' & 'mailcap', and support programs
- mount – Tools for mounting and manipulating filesystems
- nano – Small, friendly text editor inspired by Pico
- netcat – TCP/IP swiss army knife
- nginx – High performance web server
- nodejs – Node.js event-based server-side javascript engine
- openssl – Secure Sockets Layer toolkit – cryptographic utility
- patch – Apply a diff file to an original
- perl – Larry Wall's Practical Extraction and Report Language
- php (5.6, 7,0, 7.1, 7.2, 7.3, 7.4, 8.0)
- php-pgsql – PHP PostgreSQL support
- python – Interactive high-level object-oriented language
- rsync – Fast, versatile, remote (and local) file-copying tool
- sed – GNU stream editor for filtering/transforming text
- tar – GNU version of the tar archiving utility
- telnet – Basic telnet client
- unzip – De-archiver for .zip files
- vim – Vi IMproved – enhanced vi editor
- wget – Retrieves files from the web

- yarn – Fast, reliable, and secure dependency management.
- zip – Archiver for .zip files

DB CONTAINER

The following is a partial list of packages installed in the default *db* (*Alpine Linux*) container of a DDEV-Local project. For a full list of packages installed (*and version numbers*), **run** `apk info -vv | sort` from inside the container.

- bash – The GNU Bourne Again shell
- busybox – Size optimized toolbox of many common UNIX utilities
- mariadb – A fast SQL database server
- pcre – Perl-compatible regular expression library
- perl – Larry Wall's Practical Extraction and Report Language
- zlib – A compression/decompression Library

DBA CONTAINER

The following is a partial list of packages installed in the default *dba* (*Alpine Linux*) container of a DDEV-Local project. For a full list of packages installed (*and version numbers*), **run** `apk info -vv | sort` from inside the container.

- bash – The GNU Bourne Again shell
- busybox – Size optimized toolbox of many common UNIX utilities
- curl – URL retrival utility and library
- php (7.0)
- python – A high-level scripting language

- vim – Advanced text editor
- zlib – A compression/decompression Library

DDEV-LOCAL CONFIG.YAML OPTIONS

When the `ddev config` command is run, default values for most of a project's environment configuration is written to the ".ddev/config.yaml" file. You can edit this file to customize the project's environment. Consider this file your first stop when looking to customize a project's DDEV-Local configuration. This section includes a list of all the available configuration options.

- APIVersion: corresponds to the version of DDEV-Local that was used to configure the project.
- name: the project name (*machine-name format*) – this is used for the default URL for the site (`http://name.ddev.site`). If a DDEV provider is specified, this should exactly match the machine name of the site as defined by the provider.
- type: the project type (*drupal 6/7/8/0, backdrop, typo3, wordpress, laravel, magento, magento2, shopware6, php*)
- docroot: the location of the project web, or document root
- php_version: 5.6, 7.0, 7.1, 7.2 (*default*), 7.3, 7.4
- webserver_type: nginx-fpm, apache-fpm, or apache-cgi
- router_http_port: defaults to 80
- router_https_port: defaults to 443
- xdebug-enabled: defaults to false
- additional_hostnames: used to add additional .ddev.site subdomain names for the project. Wildcards can be used.
- additional_fqdns: used to add additional top-level domain names for the project
- nfs_mount_enabled: default to false

- provider: specifies a remote "provider" for the `ddev pull` command.
- upload_dir: a relative path from the project root used as the destination for the `ddev import-files` command. Defaults to "sites/default/files" for Drupal projects, "wp-content/uploads" for WordPress projects.
- working_dir: an absolute path in the *web* and/or *db* container that specifies the destination for the `ddev ssh` command as well as for commands run via `ddev exec` or via command hooks in a the ".ddev/config.yaml" file.
- omit_containers: provides the ability to configure a local project to NOT create and utilize either the *dba* or *ddev-ssh-agent* containers.
- disable_settings_management: disables DDEV-Local functionality to provide database connection (*and other*) CMS settings management (*Drupal's settings.php file, for example*).
- mariadb_version: the version of MariaDB to use in the *db* container. DDEV uses MariaDB version 10.2 as the default database container.
- mysql_version: the version of MySql to use in the *db* container. Most versions are supported. Only specify either a version of MariaDB or MySql, never both.
- host_db_port: static bind port number for *db* container.
- host_webserver_port: static bind port number for *web* container.
- webimage_extra_packages: extra Debian packages that are needed in the *web* container can be specified here instead of via a command hook. For example, if you would like to utilize the Tidy (https://www.php.net/manual/en/intro.tidy.php) library for cleaning and repairing HTML, you can add it to the *web* container by

adding the following to your project's ".ddev/config.yaml" file (*assuming your project is configured to use PHP 7.2*):

```
webimage_extra_packages: [php7.2-tidy]
```

> One method for finding available packages is to run `ddev . apt search php` from your host operating system. Another is to browse https://packages.debian.org/buster/

- dbimage_extra_packages: extra Debian packages that are needed in the *db* container can be specified here instead of via a command hook.
- composer_version: 1 or 2.
- hooks: See the *Extending DDEV-Local Commands Explained* chapter.

DDEV-LOCAL PROJECT CONFIGURATION ANATOMY

DDEV-Local creates a number of files for each project:

- /project-name
    - /.ddev
        - config.yaml – basic DDEV-Local environment configuration. Normally created via `ddev config`, can be manually edited, and edits will be respected during future "ddev config" updates.
        - config.*.yaml – local DDEV-Local configuration, normally not part of the project repository.
        - docker-compose.yaml – Docker Composer file created by DDEV-Local based on sensible

default values as well as config.yaml settings. It is not recommended for users to edit this file, as it is managed by DDEV-Local.

- docker-composer.*.yaml – user-generated Docker Compose files that normally add additional containers to the project. See the *Integrating Apache Solr with Drupal and DDEV-Local Explained* chapter for an example.
- import.yaml – When a DDEV-Local provider is specified, this DDEV-Local generated file contains metadata about the provider.
- sequelpro.spf – When the `ddev sequelpro` command is used, DDEV-Local generates this file with database connection information utilized by SequelPro.
- .gitignore – DDEV-Local generated Git ignore file to keep DDEV-Local managed files within the ".ddev/" directory out of a project's Git repository.
- /db_snapshots – When the `ddev snapshot` command is run, database snapshots are stored here.
- /import-db – Used as a Docker mount-point for the `ddev import-db` command.

ABOUT THE AUTHOR

> My name is Mike Anello and I love learning.
>
> Whether I'm learning an obscure feature of some software I've been using for years, or diving into a brand new application that is new to the scene, I still get a rush whenever I learn to do something better, faster, or (especially) more elegantly.
>
> I get a very similar rush when I can teach others something new, which explains why I've been teaching how to build Drupal sites for about a decade. In a previous career, I taught fluid dynamics, thermodynamics, and other engineering courses to undergraduates, and every time I taught, I always learned something new about the subject.

Michael Anello (@ultimike) is co-founder and vice president of DrupalEasy, a Drupal training and consulting firm based in Central Florida. Michael has been one of the main organizers of the Florida Drupal Users' Group and Florida DrupalCamps for over ten years, is a member of the Drupal Community Working Group, and also helps manage the Drupal Association's Community Cultivation Grants program.

Michael has been developing Drupal sites since 2016, specializing in module development, theming, and general site-building with a strong focus on best practices and sustainable development. Michael is also the lead trainer and curriculum developer for DrupalEasy's intensive, 12-week Drupal Career Online.

He can be heard interviewing fellow Drupal community

members, talking about current Drupal news, and highlighting new and upcoming modules on the DrupalEasy Podcast. He is an Acquia Certified Developer and a Drupal 8 core contributor.

This book also would not be possible without the help of the OSTraining team.

ARE YOU AN AUTHOR?

If you enjoy writing about the web, we'd love to talk with you.

Most publishing companies are slow, boring, inflexible and don't pay very well.

Here at OSTraining, we try to be different:

- **Fun**: We use modern publishing tools that make writing books as easy as blogging.
- **Fast**: We move quickly. Some books get written and published in less than a month.
- **Flexible**: It's easy to update your books. If technology changes in the morning, you can update your book by the afternoon.

Do you have a topic you'd love to write about? We publish books on almost all web-related topics.

Whether you want to write a short 100-page overview, or a comprehensive 500-page guide, we'd love to hear from you.

Contact us via email: books@ostraining.com.

WE WANT TO HEAR FROM YOU

Are you satisfied with your purchase of *Local Web Development With DDEV Explained*? Let us know and help us reach others who would benefit from this book.

We encourage you to share your experience. Here are two ways you can help:

- **Leave** your review on Amazon's product page of *Local Web Development With DDEV Explained*.
- **Email** your review to books@ostraining.com.

Thanks for reading *Local Web Development With DDEV Explained*. We wish you the best in your future endeavors with the software.

SPONSOR AN OSTRAINING BOOK

Is your company interested in sponsoring an OSTraining book? Our books are some of the world's best-selling guides to the software they cover.

People love to read our books and learn about new web design topics.

Why not reach those people? Partner with us to showcase your company to thousands of web developers.
We have partnered with Acquia, Pantheon, Nexcess, GoDaddy, InMotion, GlowHost and Ecwid to provide sponsored training to millions of people.

If you want to learn more, visit https://marketing.ostraining.com or email us at books@ostraining.com.

www.ingramcontent.com/pod-product-compliance
Lightning Source LLC
Chambersburg PA
CBHW071534220526
45469CB00003B/778